JOSH GIBSON

JOSH GIBSON

John B. Holway

CHELSEA HOUSE PUBLISHERS

New York   Philadelphia

Chelsea House Publishers

Editorial Director Richard Rennert
Executive Managing Editor Karyn Gullen Browne
Copy Chief Robin James
Picture Editor Adrian G. Allen
Creative Director Robert Mitchell
Art Director Joan Ferrigno
Production Manager Sallye Scott

Black Americans of Achievement
Senior Editor Philip Koslow

Staff for JOSH GIBSON
Editorial Assistant Sydra Mallery
Senior Designer Marjorie Zaum
Picture Researcher Lisa Kirchner
Cover Illustrator Daniel O'Leary

First Printing

1 3 5 7 9 8 6 4 2

Library of Congress Cataloging-in-Publication Data
Holway, John B.
Josh Gibson: John B. Holway.
    p. cm. — (Black Americans of achievement)
  Includes bibliographical references and index.
  ISBN   0-7910-1872-5.
            0-7910-1901-2 (pbk.)
  1. Gibson, Josh, 1911–1947—Juvenile literature. 2. Baseball
players—United States—Biography—Juvenile literature. [1.
Gibson, Josh, 1911–1947. 2. Baseball players. 3.
Afro-Americans— Biography.] I. Title. II. Series.
GV865.G53H35 1995   94-45247
796.357.357'092—dc20   CIP
[B]   AC

Frontispiece: *Josh Gibson
during the 1930s, when he
starred with the Homestead
Grays of the Negro National
League.*

CONTENTS

BLACK AMERICANS OF ACHIEVEMENT

HENRY AARON
baseball great

KAREEM ABDUL-JABBAR
basketball great

RALPH ABERNATHY
civil rights leader

ALVIN AILEY
choreographer

MUHAMMAD ALI
heavyweight champion

RICHARD ALLEN
*religious leader and
social activist*

MAYA ANGELOU
author

LOUIS ARMSTRONG
musician

ARTHUR ASHE
tennis great

JOSEPHINE BAKER
entertainer

JAMES BALDWIN
author

BENJAMIN BANNEKER
scientist and mathematician

AMIRI BARAKA
poet and playwright

COUNT BASIE
bandleader and composer

ROMARE BEARDEN
artist

JAMES BECKWOURTH
frontiersman

MARY MCLEOD BETHUNE
educator

JULIAN BOND
civil rights leader and politician

GWENDOLYN BROOKS
poet

JIM BROWN
football great

STOKELY CARMICHAEL
civil rights leader

GEORGE WASHINGTON
CARVER
botanist

RAY CHARLES
musician

CHARLES CHESNUTT
author

JOHN COLTRANE
musician

BILL COSBY
entertainer

PAUL CUFFE
merchant and abolitionist

COUNTEE CULLEN
poet

BENJAMIN DAVIS, SR., AND
BENJAMIN DAVIS, JR.
military leaders

MILES DAVIS
musician

SAMMY DAVIS, JR.
entertainer

FATHER DIVINE
religious leader

FREDERICK DOUGLASS
abolitionist editor

CHARLES DREW
physician

W. E. B. DU BOIS
scholar and activist

PAUL LAURENCE DUNBAR
poet

KATHERINE DUNHAM
dancer and choreographer

DUKE ELLINGTON
bandleader and composer

RALPH ELLISON
author

JULIUS ERVING
basketball great

JAMES FARMER
civil rights leader

ELLA FITZGERALD
singer

MARCUS GARVEY
black nationalist leader

JOSH GIBSON
baseball great

DIZZY GILLESPIE
musician

WHOOPI GOLDBERG
entertainer

ALEX HALEY
author

PRINCE HALL
social reformer

MATTHEW HENSON
explorer

CHESTER HIMES
author

BILLIE HOLIDAY
singer

LENA HORNE
entertainer

LANGSTON HUGHES
poet

ZORA NEALE HURSTON
author

JESSE JACKSON
civil rights leader and politician

MICHAEL JACKSON
entertainer

JACK JOHNSON
heavyweight champion

JAMES WELDON JOHNSON
author

MAGIC JOHNSON
basketball great

SCOTT JOPLIN
composer

BARBARA JORDAN
politician

MICHAEL JORDAN
basketball great

CORETTA SCOTT KING
civil rights leader

MARTIN LUTHER KING, JR.
civil rights leader

LEWIS LATIMER
scientist

SPIKE LEE
filmmaker

CARL LEWIS
champion athlete

JOE LOUIS
heavyweight champion

RONALD MCNAIR
astronaut

MALCOLM X
militant black leader

THURGOOD MARSHALL
Supreme Court justice

TONI MORRISON
author

ELIJAH MUHAMMAD
religious leader

EDDIE MURPHY
entertainer

JESSE OWENS
champion athlete

SATCHEL PAIGE
baseball great

CHARLIE PARKER
musician

GORDON PARKS
photographer

ROSA PARKS
civil rights leader

SIDNEY POITIER
actor

ADAM CLAYTON
POWELL, JR.
political leader

COLIN POWELL
military leader

LEONTYNE PRICE
opera singer

A. PHILIP RANDOLPH
labor leader

PAUL ROBESON
singer and actor

JACKIE ROBINSON
baseball great

DIANA ROSS
entertainer

BILL RUSSELL
basketball great

JOHN RUSSWURM
publisher

SOJOURNER TRUTH
antislavery activist

HARRIET TUBMAN
antislavery activist

NAT TURNER
slave revolt leader

DENMARK VESEY
slave revolt leader

ALICE WALKER
author

MADAM C. J. WALKER
entrepreneur

BOOKER T. WASHINGTON
educator and racial spokesman

IDA WELLS-BARNETT
civil rights leader

WALTER WHITE
civil rights leader

OPRAH WINFREY
entertainer

STEVIE WONDER
musician

RICHARD WRIGHT
author

ON ACHIEVEMENT

Coretta Scott King

BEFORE YOU BEGIN this book, I hope you will ask yourself what the word *excellence* means to you. I think that it's a question we should all ask, and keep asking as we grow older and change. Because the truest answer to it should never change. When you think of excellence, perhaps you think of success at work; or of becoming wealthy; or meeting the right person, getting married, and having a good family life.

Those important goals are worth striving for, but there is a better way to look at excellence. As Martin Luther King, Jr., said in one of his last sermons, "I want you to be first in love. I want you to be first in moral excellence. I want you to be first in generosity. If you want to be important, wonderful. If you want to be great, wonderful. But recognize that he who is greatest among you shall be your servant."

My husband, Martin Luther King, Jr., knew that the true meaning of achievement is service. When I met him, in 1952, he was already ordained as a Baptist preacher and was working toward a doctoral degree at Boston University. I was studying at the New England Conservatory and dreamed of accomplishments in music. We married a year later, and after I graduated the following year we moved to Montgomery, Alabama. We didn't know it then, but our notions of achievement were about to undergo a dramatic change.

You may have read or heard about what happened next. What began with the boycott of a local bus line grew into a national movement, and by the time he was assassinated in 1968 my husband had fashioned a black movement powerful enough to shatter forever the practice of racial segregation. What you may not have read about is where he got his method for resisting injustice without compromising his religious beliefs.

He adopted the strategy of nonviolence from a man of a different race, who lived in a different country, and even practiced a different religion. The man was Mahatma Gandhi, the great leader of India, who devoted his life to serving humanity in the spirit of love and nonviolence. It was in these principles that Martin discovered his method for social reform. More than anything else, those two principles were the key to his achievements.

This book is about black Americans who served society through the excellence of their achievements. It forms a part of the rich history of black men and women in America—a history of stunning accomplishments in every field of human endeavor, from literature and art to science, industry, education, diplomacy, athletics, jurisprudence, even polar exploration.

Not all of the people in this history had the same ideals, but I think you will find something that all of them had in common. Like Martin Luther King, Jr., they all decided to become "drum majors" and serve humanity. In that principle—whether it was expressed in books, inventions, or song—they found something outside themselves to use as a goal and a guide. Something that showed them a way to serve others, instead of only living for themselves.

Reading the stories of these courageous men and women not only helps us discover the principles that we will use to guide our own lives but also teaches us about our black heritage and about America itself. It is crucial for us to know the heroes and heroines of our history and to realize that the price we paid in our struggle for equality in America was dear. But we must also understand that we have gotten as far as we have partly because America's democratic system and ideals made it possible.

We are still struggling with racism and prejudice. But the great men and women in this series are a tribute to the spirit of our democratic ideals and the system in which they have flourished. And that makes their stories special and worth knowing. ❦

1

A CLOUT FOR THE AGES

❧

Josh Gibson poses for photographers before a Negro league contest during the 1930s. Standing 6 feet 1 and weighing 215 pounds, the powerful Gibson was one of the most fearsome sluggers in baseball history.

THE YOUNG CATCHER pulled up the sleeves of his striped white Homestead Grays uniform, revealing muscular brown biceps. Eighteen-year-old Josh Gibson had played only two months in the Negro leagues, and here he was in a championship series.

He tapped the plate with his bat and looked out at the towering triple-decked stands of Yankee Stadium, the largest, most famous baseball palace in America in 1930. With the stands looming as high as a 10-story building and the left-center-field fence measuring 467 feet from home plate, Yankee Stadium was a daunting sight for a right-handed hitter. No man had ever hit a ball out of it, not even baseball's most famous slugger, Babe Ruth.

Standing at the plate, Gibson eyed Broadway Connie Rector, the pitcher for the home team Lincoln Giants. Rector was a crafty 30-year-old veteran with the most tantalizing slow ball in the Negro leagues; he stood casually on the mound, looking in at the plate with a grin, letting the youngster feel the pressure.

This championship series was an entirely different event from the World Series that was to be played between the Philadelphia Athletics and the St. Louis Cardinals the following month. In the upcoming series, the players would all be white. In this one, they were all African Americans.

Back in 1930, major league baseball was completely segregated. Black youngsters dreamed not of joining the Yankees or Dodgers or Red Sox but of starring with some of the great black teams of the Negro leagues, such as the Grays, the Kansas City Monarchs, the Chicago American Giants, or the Lincoln Giants.

During the regular season, the Grays had thrashed the Monarchs, considered the kings of the West, in 10 out of 11 games. The Lincolns then challenged the Grays to a 10-game series to determine the championship of the East. When Gibson came to bat against Rector in Game 7, on September 27, the Grays enjoyed a 4–2 lead in the series. Against the Monarchs, Gibson had batted only .242 with a single home run. But against the Lincolns he had suddenly come to life with two long home runs, a triple, and a double.

Luther Farrell, the Lincolns starter in Game 7, seemed to have Gibson's number, holding the young slugger hitless in four at-bats. Rector, called in from the bullpen in the ninth, posed a unique challenge. His best pitch was a change of pace that came up to the plate at three different speeds. "The first one was slow," recalled first baseman George Giles of the St. Louis Stars. "The second one walked up to the plate. The third one crawled up there." Batters grew frantic waiting for the ball to arrive so they could swing. If they did hit it, they had to supply all their own power.

Rector calmly waited on the mound, hoping that Gibson would grow nervous and overanxious. At last, he slowly went into his windup and sent a pitch floating toward the plate. Gibson did not lunge at the ball as Rector had hoped. Instead, he held back, timed the speed of the ball perfectly, and then unleashed his bat.

The ball shot deep into left-center field on a long, low arc. Where it landed is—and always will be—a subject of dispute. Three men who were on the field that day gave three different accounts. William "Judy" Johnson of the Grays said Gibson's blast carried over the grandstand roof and out of the park. Lincolns pitcher Bill Holland recalled that the ball soared higher than the roof but came down and struck the back wall of the bullpen that separated the grandstand from the center-field bleachers—two feet higher, and it would have left the stadium entirely. The Lincolns catcher, Larry Brown, claimed that the ball passed under the roof before hitting the back wall, 505 feet from home plate. Gibson himself later said, "I hit the ball on a line into the bullpen in deep left field."

Since that day, only two players have come close to hitting a ball off the bullpen wall—Dave Winfield of the New York Yankees and Doug DeCinces of the California Angels. But neither one could duplicate the feat of 18-year-old Josh Gibson on that September afternoon in the black World Series of 1930. ◖◗•

During a championship series against the Lincoln Giants in September 1930, Gibson clouted one of the most colossal home runs in the history of Yankee Stadium. According to one eyewitness, the ball struck the back wall of the left-field bullpen (indicated by arrow), about 505 feet from home plate.

2

"WHY, HE'S ONLY A BOY!"

❦

JOSHUA GIBSON WAS born on December 21, 1911, in the dusty little town of Buena Vista, Georgia, about 100 miles south of Atlanta. As a future baseball player, he could not have been born at a worse time. His career, which extended from 1930 to 1946, was destined to coincide with the last 17 years of segregated baseball, a 60-year-long era that began in 1887 and ended in 1947 when Jackie Robinson joined the Brooklyn Dodgers. Gibson's birthday also doomed him to play most of his career during the worst economic slump in American history, the Great Depresssion of 1930–39.

The world that young Josh was born into provided him with few advantages. His parents, Mark and Nancy Gibson, worked as sharecroppers—small farmers who worked a plot of ground owned by a white landlord and were paid for their labor with a share of the crops they raised. Like most black sharecroppers in the rural South, the Gibsons worked long and hard to support their growing family: a second son, Mark junior, was born three years after Josh, and a daughter, Annie, followed three years after Mark.

In the years following the outbreak of World War I in 1914, industries in the North began to expand, and many blacks left the South, seeking higher wages and better living conditions in northern cities such as Chicago, Cleveland, and Pittsburgh. In 1921,

A farmer hauls a load of hay during the early years of the 20th century. When Josh Gibson was born in Buena Vista, Georgia, in 1911, his family struggled to earn a living as sharecroppers, working a plot of land that belonged to someone else.

when Josh was 10, Mark Gibson joined the tide of migrants. Traveling to Pittsburgh, Pennsylvania, where a number of his relatives had settled, he found a job in the Carnegie-Illinois steel mill. By 1924, he had saved enough money to send for his wife and children. In his book *Only the Ball Was White*, Robert Peterson quotes Gibson as saying, "The greatest gift Dad gave me was to get me out of the South."

The Gibsons settled in a black neighborhood called Pleasant Valley, located on Pittsburgh's North Side. After grade school, Josh enrolled in a vocational school to study the electrician's trade. But he really preferred swimming and track and field, in which he won several ribbons. He also played baseball for the Pleasant Valley Red Sox, a local sandlot team.

When Josh was 16, he went to work in the steel mills himself. He also played third base for an amateur team known as the Gimbels A.C., digging ground balls out of the rock-strewn playground fields and hitting balls halfway up the hillside. Harold Tinker, the manager of a semipro team known as the Craw-

An aerial view of Pittsburgh's Carnegie-Illinois steel mill, where Josh Gibson's father worked during the 1920s. "The greatest gift Dad gave me was to get me out of the South," Josh later remarked.

ford Colored Giants, saw the youngster play and decided to recruit him. "Josh," he asked, "don't you want to play with a real team?"

"Yes sir," the boy replied. "I guess so."

Gibson played for the Crawford Colored Giants throughout 1929 and 1930. He did not get much money for his efforts. Admission to the games was free, and the team passed the hat among the spectators, who chipped in five cents apiece so that the players could go home with a few dollars for their day's work. The money came in handy for Gibson, because at the age of 17 he had married his girlfriend, Helen.

The Crawfords liked Gibson's arm and made him a catcher. "You could put your hands on him and feel him," Tinker recalled. "Man, he was hard. His muscles were hard. He wasn't big, but he was a sinewy type. He was built like metal. If you run into him, it was like you run into a wall." According to Tinker, Gibson could blast balls "out on Bedford Avenue and up on the hospital." The *Pittsburgh Courier,* a black newspaper, began to notice Gibson and published accounts of his most spectacular home runs.

If Gibson had been white, he might have dreamed of playing for the hometown Pittsburgh Pirates of the National League, who featured outfielders Paul and Lloyd Waner and third baseman Pie Traynor. But with the color line firmly entrenched in baseball, Gibson's greatest ambition was to play for the Homestead Grays of the Negro National League.

The history of black baseball goes back at least to 1867, when two black amateur teams, the Philadelphia Excelsiors and the Brooklyn Uniques, played for the black championship of America. (The Excelsiors won by a score of 42–37.) The first black professional player was Bud Fowler of Cooperstown, New York, who played in the white Northwestern League. According to Robert Peterson, Fowler was one of 60

Moses Fleetwood Walker (seated at left) and Welday Wilberforce Walker, shown here with other members of the 1884 Toledo team of the Northwestern League. Fleet Walker, as he was known, had joined the team the year before, becoming the first black professional baseball player in U.S. history.

black players in white organized baseball before the turn of the 20th century.

The first blacks to play major league baseball were the Walker brothers: Moses Fleetwood and Welday Wilberforce. Graduates of Oberlin College in Ohio, the Walkers played in 1884 for Toledo in the American Association, then a major league. Though Jackie Robinson is credited with breaking baseball's color line in the 20th century, Moses and Welday Walker were the first black major leaguers in baseball history, preceding Robinson by 63 years. Their stint was short-lived, however: when Toledo dropped out of the league in 1885, the Walkers returned to the minors.

In 1887, four other blacks joined the Walkers in the minors. Frank Grant, a small second baseman, batted .366 for Buffalo in the International League, the top minor league. George Stovey won 33 games for Newark in the same league, and Robert Higgins had a 20-7 record for Syracuse. In addition, Sol White batted .381 in the Ohio State League.

Fans outside the South were generally tolerant of the black players, but they were not accepted by their white peers. Indeed, white players were said to have invented the feet-first slide so that they could spike Fowler and Grant. The two black players responded by devising the first shin guards, which were made out of wood. The whites then filed their spikes to razor sharpness in order to split the shin guards. Finally, Grant brought the spiking war to a halt by moving to the outfield. But he still had to contend with white pitchers who threw at his head, and in 1889 he left the league altogether.

Some white players refused to play with blacks or have their pictures taken with them. When Stovey was scheduled to pitch an exhibition against the Chicago White Stockings of the National League, Chicago star Cap Anson reportedly growled, "Get that nigger off the field." The major league New York Giants wanted to buy Stovey, but Anson reportedly blocked the sale. That same year, the St. Louis Browns players threatened to strike rather than play an exhibition against a black club. One by one, the black players were eased out of white baseball and onto segregated Negro teams.

The first black professional team may have been the Philadelphia Orions in 1882. The best black team of that era was the Cuban Giants, created in 1885. The players were not Cubans but black Americans who worked as waiters at the Argyle Hotel on Long Island, New York and were organized into a team by Frank Thompson, the Argyle's headwaiter. The players' salaries ranged from $12 to $18 a week. In the fall of 1885, the Cuban Giants played the best white team in the country, the Detroit Tigers, and lost by a score of 4–2. Eventually, the Cuban Giants signed Grant, Stovey, and other black stars from the white minor leagues. By the late 1880s, other professional Negro teams had sprung up all over the country, and the *Sporting News* asserted, "There are players among these colored men that are equal to any white players on the ballfield."

Black players almost cracked the major league color barrier at the beginning of the 20th century. In 1901, manager John McGraw of the Baltimore Orioles in the American League tried to sign a black player, second baseman Charlie "Cincy" Grant. Grant was light skinned, and McGraw tried to pass him off as a Cherokee Indian, giving him the name Charlie Tokohama. However, during an exhibition game in Chicago, hundreds of black fans turned out to cheer the man they called "Our boy, Charlie Grant." Chicago White Stockings owner Charles Comiskey got wind of the incident and raised so much commotion about the signing of Grant that McGraw was forced to drop the idea. The following year, when he became the manager of the New York Giants, McGraw hired a black pitcher, Andrew "Rube" Foster, but Foster was only asked to teach Giants star Christy Mathewson to throw a screwball.

As the new century got under way, the black teams continued to prosper. In 1903, Sol White's Philadelphia Giants beat Foster's Cuban X Giants in the first Negro World Series, the same year that the Boston Red Stockings and Pittsburgh Pirates were playing the first major league World Series.

Many great black teams followed. Among them were Foster's Chicago American Giants, the New York Lincoln Giants, the Indianapolis ABCs, the Royal Giants, the Atlantic City Bacharach Giants, the Philadelphia Hilldales, and the All Nations of Kansas City.

In 1920, Foster organized eight western teams into the Negro National League: Kansas City, St. Louis, Detroit, Indianapolis, Columbus, Cincinnati,

The Cuban Giants, shown here in an unusual blend of photography and line drawing, were the best of the early black professional teams. After watching one of their games in 1888, a white reporter wrote, "There are players among these colored men that are equal to any white players on the ballfield."

and Chicago (two teams). Three years later Ed Bolden, owner of the Hilldales, formed the Eastern Colored League, which consisted of the Brooklyn Royal Giants, the Lincoln Giants, the Bacharach Giants, the Baltimore Black Sox, the Hilldale Club, and a Cuban team.

But the best team of all did not belong to either league: they were the Grays of Homestead, Pennsylvania, a suburb of Pittsburgh. The Grays owner, Cumberland "Cum" Posey, was a native of Homestead. One of his grandfathers had been a slave in the South; the other had fought in the Union army during the Civil War. Posey's father was the first licensed black ship's pilot on the Ohio River and later owned a fleet of coal barges. His mother was the first African American to graduate from Ohio State University. Posey himself attended Penn State and Duquesne universities, but he was more interested in playing golf and basketball and dropped out of both schools.

In 1909, Posey joined the Grays, a local steel mill baseball team. Before long, he had convinced them to charge admission and to pay the players a few dollars per game. In the winter, Posey played guard on the Loendi Big Five, one of the best early basketball teams in America, and he was hailed as one of the top players in the country. The team played white teams like the New York Celtics for $75 a game and in 1919 claimed the national championship.

Meanwhile, the Grays played other black big league teams in addition to white semipro squads in Pennsylvania, Ohio, and West Virginia. They also played teams of white major leaguers who went on barnstorming tours during the off-season. According to unofficial records, the Grays had their finest season in 1926, when they reportedly won 140 games and lost only 13. By remaining independent, they made more money than they could have made in either of the Negro leagues.

By 1930, the Grays' biggest star was first baseman–manager Oscar Charleston, a barrel-chested

Gibson (standing, fourth from right) poses with other members of the 1931 Homestead Grays. Cumberland "Cum" Posey, the team's owner, is standing on the far left; Oscar Charleston, the great center fielder, is second from the right in the back row.

outfielder who may have been the best player in black baseball. (John McGraw called Charleston the best player he had ever seen, black or white.) Charleston was so strong that he could reportedly wrench the steering wheel off an automobile or loosen a baseball's cover with one hand, and he was so fearless that he once pulled the hood off a member of the Ku Klux Klan, a racist organization that tried to intimidate blacks throughout the South.

Born in 1896, the same year as Babe Ruth, Charleston ran away from home at the age of 15 and joined the army. He honed his baseball skills while serving in the Philippines, and upon his discharge in 1915, he joined the Indianapolis ABCs. Charleston played with the same savage, slashing drive as Ty Cobb, the greatest white player of the era. Both were lightning fast and played for blood. At bat, both men ripped the ball to all fields. (Cobb's lifetime batting average was .367, the highest in major league history, while Charleston's career mark was .357.) But unlike Cobb, Charleston swung for the fences and often reached them—he ranks fourth on the all-time home run list of the Negro leagues. In the field, moreover, Charleston was far superior to Cobb. Like the great Boston Red Sox center fielder Tris Speaker, he could stand nearly behind second base and still outrun a long line drive. No wonder, then, that when white sportswriters called Charleston "the black Cobb," black writers replied that Cobb was "the white Charleston." Cobb was among the first group of inductees to the Baseball Hall of Fame in 1936. After the decision was made to include Negro leaguers in Cooperstown, Charleston took his rightful place beside Cobb in 1976.

The Grays also boasted the best pitcher in the Negro leagues, Smoky Joe Williams. A big Texan whose mother was part Indian, Williams reputedly got his nickname when he hurled a no-hitter against

Smoky Joe Williams, finishing his career with the Grays during Gibson's early years, threw as hard as any pitcher in baseball history. During the prime of his career, it was not unusual for the rangy Texan to strike out 20 batters in a single game.

McGraw's pennant-winning 1917 Giants, striking out 20 batters: as Giants outfielder Ross Youngs trotted off the field after the game, he slapped Williams on the backside and exclaimed, "That was a hell of a game, Smoky." Williams was often compared to Walter Johnson of the Washington Senators, the dominant pitcher of the American League. In 1918, Williams and Johnson hooked up in a pitchers' duel, which Williams won 1–0 on a home run by Oscar Charleston. In all, Williams pitched 27 games against white major leaguers, winning 20 and losing 7. His victims included Hall of Famers Johnson, Grover Alexander, Chief Bender, Rube Marquard, and Waite Hoyt. In 1952, Williams was voted the greatest pitcher in Negro league history, defeating Satchel Paige by one vote.

Gibson's association with the Grays began during a dismal time in American history. Following the disastrous stock market crash of 1929, factories were shut down. Unemployed men formed long lines wherever there was a chance of finding work, while others stood on street corners selling apples or pencils for a few cents. There was no unemployment insurance or any government welfare payments to help the needy. Farmers lost their farms because they could not pay the mortgage, and they streamed to the cities to join the other unemployed men already there.

Like almost everyone in the country, the black baseball teams were barely scraping by. Players made a few hundred dollars a month for a four- or five-month season. They slept in buses, sometimes played three games on Sunday, and often passed the hat around the stands to collect nickels and dimes from the equally broke spectators. To make matters worse for the Gibsons, they were expecting a baby.

In the midst of desperate economic conditions, baseball and other forms of public entertainment helped people forget their problems for a little while.

Sports promoters continually searched for ways to attract fans, and the 1930 season featured the first night games in the history of organized baseball leagues.

On the humid night of July 25, Gibson was sitting in the stands at Pittsburgh's Forbes Field along with thousands of other fans, watching the first night game ever played in Pittsburgh. The Grays had rented the park, the home of the Pirates, for a contest with the Kansas City Monarchs, who traveled with a portable lighting system.

The lights were far dimmer than those of modern-day ballparks, creating a hazard for hitters and catchers, especially with the hard-throwing Smoky Joe Williams on the mound. The Grays catcher got crossed up on one of Williams's deliveries and wound up with a split finger. According to Grays manager William "Judy" Johnson, the team's backup catcher, who was playing the outfield, refused to go behind the plate. Johnson had noticed Gibson in the stands and asked Cum Posey to approach him. "So Cum asked Josh would he catch," Johnson recalled, "and Josh said, 'Yeah, oh yeah!' We had to hold the game up until he went into the clubhouse and got a uniform. And that's what started him out with the Homestead Grays."

Gibson went hitless in two at-bats. He was confused by foul balls, and he caught pitches like a "boxer," knocking them down, then picking them up. But he must have handled Williams well, because the Grays won the game, and Gibson won a job.

Gibson's fortunes appeared to have taken a turn for the better, but his good luck in joining the Grays was soon marred by tragedy. In late August, Helen Gibson died while giving birth to twins, Helen and Josh junior. Josh senior did not even have time to grieve. The Grays were embarking on a cross-country barnstorming tour with the Monarchs, and he had no other way of making a living. He left the newborn twins with Helen's mother and sister, packed his bags, and went on the road.

The Grays traveled seven men to a car, storing their clothes in racks on the sides and their equipment in a big box on the rear.

They barnstormed with the Monarchs, the best black team in the West, showing off the portable lights at every stop. At Hershey, Pennsylvania, an overflow crowd literally knocked the fences down to get in, then stood idly about, looking in awe at the lights.

Despite the popularity of the tour, Gibson struggled at the plate. The dim lighting contributed to his problems, and he was probably still in shock from his wife's sudden death. The Monarchs hurlers held him to a .242 average. His fielding also suffered. He dropped a lot of pitches, and he said high fouls "made him drunk." Johnson spent long hours working with Gibson. He taught the boy how to read the spin on foul pop-ups, pointing out that the ball carries toward the stands on the way up and drifts back toward the field on the way down. He showed Josh how to catch every pitch, legal and illegal, the black pitchers threw—spitballs, scuffed balls, and "vaseline" balls. By the time Johnson was finished teaching him, Gibson could at least knock the ball down, even if he could not always catch it.

After each game, the young catcher would come to the manager's office.

"How'd I do today?" he'd ask.

"Josh, you caught a real good game today," Johnson would answer, "except . . . "

After hearing Johnson's criticism, Gibson would reply, "Well, I'll work on that tomorrow."

Recalling those conversations years later, Johnson shook his head with admiration. "That boy was game," he said. "I've seen the time Josh had his finger split and tied a piece of tape around it and played just as though nothing had happened. He really wanted to learn."

One thing no one had to teach Gibson was how to throw. According to old-timers, nobody threw quicker or straighter than Gibson, and he threw a "light" ball that the infielders loved to catch.

In Kansas City on August 7, Gibson took part in one of the greatest pitching duels ever seen in baseball, black or white, when Joe Williams hooked up against Chet Brewer of the Monarchs. Williams was strictly a fireballer, whereas Brewer was a "sandpaper" artist who could cut the cover of the ball and make it do tricks. For 11 innings the two dueled without yielding a run. Brewer allowed four hits, Williams only one. Brewer struck out 19 batters, 12 in a row at one point; Williams fanned 27 of the 34 men he faced.

During the game, Gibson served notice that he was not going to be intimidated by anyone. As Willie Wells of the St. Louis Stars later put it, the early Negro league pitchers threw at the hitters "like they were a rat or something." Pitchers were known to growl at batters, "Hold still—how'm I gonna hit you if you don't hold still?" In self-defense, Wells obtained a coal miner's hard hat, removed the lamp from the front, and wore it to the plate, thus inventing baseball's first batting helmet.

Brewer remembered that "the first time up I got Josh's cap bill—don't know how I missed his head." Brewer then walked halfway to the plate. "Missed you this time," he called, "but I'm gonna get you next time."

"You see this bat?" Gibson retorted. "The first time you hit me, I'm gonna hit you!"

Finally, in the 12th, the Grays scored a run on a walk, an error, and a fluke hit and won the game 1–0. The 18-year-old Gibson had caught one of the classic

During the 1930s, one of the great attractions in black baseball was the portable lighting system used by the Kansas City Monarchs. On July 25, 1930, when the Monarchs and the Grays played the first night game ever seen in Pittsburgh, 18-year-old Josh Gibson made his Negro league debut.

games of all time. Gibson hit his first home run in St. Louis on September 6 in a game against the Stars, who featured James "Cool Papa" Bell, perhaps the fastest man in the history of the game, and George "Mule" Suttles, the powerful Alabama coal miner who had led the Negro leagues in home runs in 1926. Gibson hit his homer against the ace of the St. Louis staff, Ted "Big Florida" Trent. Trent had a legendary curve that some players said could go around a barrel. He once struck out the New York Giants' Bill Terry, a .341 lifetime hitter, four times in one night.

The left-field foul line at the St. Louis park was short, estimated at only 250 feet, but the center-field fence was almost 500 feet from home plate. Two trolley-car barns stood beyond the fences, one in left field and one in left-center. Gibson's blast off Trent sailed over the second barn. The Stars players could hardly believe what they had seen. "Bring him up close," Bell said after the game, "let us look at him." Then the fleet-footed outfielder gasped, "Why, he's only a boy!"

In all, the two teams played 12 games on the tour, and the Grays won 11 of them. There were no formal leagues in that year because of the depression, so no black World Series was held, as it had been in other years. But the Grays considered themselves the kings of the East. Only one team challenged them, the Lincoln Giants. The Lincolns were led by the beloved John Henry "Pop" Lloyd, perhaps one of the two best shortstops of all time, along with Honus Wagner of the white major leagues. In right field they had Charlie "Chino" Smith, a scrappy little hitter, who won the batting championship of the East with a .468 average.

Each team carried only about 14 men, compared to 25 on the white big league teams. The series opened with a doubleheader in Pittsburgh, where the Grays won the opener handily, 9–1. In Game 2,

Gibson hit a long home run over the center-field fence, 457 feet away, as the Grays won a 10-inning slugfest, 17–16. (Only three other men have ever equaled Gibson's feat: his teammate Oscar Charleston, Mickey Mantle of the New York Yankees, and Dick Stuart of the Pirates.) That night, the exhausted players piled into their bus for a long ride to New York and another doubleheader the next afternoon. This time the Lincolns beat Joe Williams in the opener, but the Grays came back to take the nightcap, as Gibson hit a key double off Luther Farrell.

In Game 5, which was played in Philadelphia, Gibson bashed the longest home run ever seen in Bigler Field, to help win the game 13–7. The Lincolns captured Game 6, sending the series back to Yankee Stadium, where Gibson walloped his famous home run deep into the left-field bullpen.

The Grays went on to win the series, splitting a Sunday doubleheader in New York. Gibson batted .368 for the nine games. Then the players climbed into their bus and crossed the Hudson River to Newark, New Jersey, to play their third game of the day—this one against a white minor league team, the Newark Bears. The Grays may have been the greatest black team in America, but they still had to meet their payroll. ◄❂►

3

DEPRESSION DAYS

WHILE THE DEPRESSION deepened across the United States, Gibson went to spring training with the Grays in March 1931 in Hot Springs, Arkansas. Despite his personal sorrows, he was always high-spirited around his teammates, and they all liked him. "He was the biggest kid you ever saw in your life," Judy Johnson recalled. "Like he was 12 or 13 years old. Oh, he was jolly *all* the time. You had to love him."

The older players nicknamed Gibson "Big Boy." "All those home runs never did go to his head," one player said. "Some stars, they think they're greater than anybody else. But Josh was always the same."

"He was just a big overgrown kid," Grays outfielder Ted Page agreed. He and Gibson were close in age and spent time together off the field. When the older players went out drinking or partying, Gibson and Page would go to an ice cream parlor. "I remember one game," Page recalled. "We went back to the hotel, and there was a ball game in session behind the hotel. He went right out there and got in the game, and he played just as hard with those kids as he had in the two games that afternoon."

On the field, the classic Gibson swing was already evident. "He was as strong as two men," said Monte Irvin, who later played for the New York Giants. "He had a fluid swing, like Ted Williams."

Gibson demonstrates his powerful and compact swing for photographers during the early 1930s. Unlike most home run hitters, Gibson rarely struck out and had little trouble hitting breaking pitches.

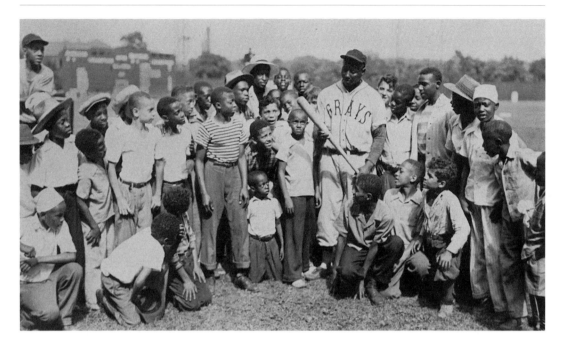

Gibson gives some baseball pointers to a group of young admirers. During his early years, Gibson was so in love with baseball that he would sometimes join a sandlot game after playing with the Grays. "He was the biggest kid you ever saw in your life," said his manager, Judy Johnson.

When Babe Ruth missed a pitch, he sometimes ended up falling over from the force of his swing. But Gibson's swing was short and quick. He stood straight up with his legs apart. His bat remained still until he uncoiled it. Like Ted Williams, he could wait on the ball until the last moment, seeming to hit it out of the catcher's mitt. One writer claimed that Gibson's bat "blurred through the strike zone like a swarm of bees."

Unlike many sluggers, Gibson hit the ball where it was pitched and seldom struck out. Most home run hitters have trouble with curve balls, but Gibson loved them. He would often let two fastballs go by for strikes and then hit the 0-2 curve. He could be fooled by an outside curve and still hit the ball over the right-field fence with one hand on the bat, and he could pull any inside pitch over the fence in left. As one pitcher muttered, "If you threw it outside, he'd kill the ball. If you threw it inside, he'd kill the third baseman."

Infielders learned to sidestep his ground-ball smashes like matadors waving their capes at a bull. When they managed to stop the ball they had to hurry their throws, because Gibson could also run, even after he filled out to 6 feet 1 and 215 pounds. He once hit a home run on a scorching grounder that went through the infield and scooted between the outfielders. Before they could chase the ball down, one player recalled, "Josh was sitting on the bench."

Gibson's home run production is all the more impressive in light of the conditions he played under. When the Grays went up north, they played their home games in Pittsburgh's Forbes Field, the hardest park in the National League to hit homers in, with a left-field foul line 365 feet from home. Also, the Negro leagues did not use major league balls; they played with a less expensive ball that did not carry as far. "It's a good thing," said one of Gibson's teammates. "Otherwise Josh would probably have killed someone."

The Grays were a hard-hitting club. Second baseman George Scales batted .393. Oscar Charleston hit .380. The third baseman, burly Jud Wilson, hit .367. The 19-year-old Gibson fit right in. He batted .372 and slugged 6 homers in the 32 games the Grays played against other Negro league teams.

In fact, there was no formal Negro league in 1931. The depression had taken its toll, and the teams operated independently, taking games wherever they could find them. When the owners could not pay the bills, the players took over and passed the hat among the patrons. They deducted team expenses, such as gas for the bus or the cars, then split whatever was left among themselves.

Although they played only one or two Negro league teams a week, the Grays also played industrial teams all around the Pittsburgh area, traveling throughout Pennsylvania, West Virginia, Ohio, and

Kentucky. According to Eric "Ric" Roberts, a sports-writer from the *Pittsburgh Courier* who followed the Grays, Gibson hit a total of 75 home runs in 1931 and batted .608. Because there were no official box scores for the games between the Grays and the semipro teams, there is no way of knowing exactly how many home runs Gibson really hit.

As always, the schedule was brutal. The players traveled by bus, trying to sleep in their seats overnight before tumbling out to play the next day. On Sundays, they often played three games—two Negro league games in the afternoon and a game against a semipro team at night. "Man, you're spent," one player recalled. "You try to save a little from the day games, then you go out to play tonight's game; you're stiff, tired, and you're just forcing yourself. We logged 30,000 miles one summer. Of course you get tired around July or August. The people didn't know what we went through. They'd see us dragging around. They didn't know we'd ridden all night getting there."

The Negro leaguers had no trainers to give them rubdowns or to tape their aching legs. Every player had to take care of himself. There were few reserves, so players had to play through their injuries. Besides, with so many hungry players waiting to take their jobs, they were afraid to miss any games.

Weekday games against the semipro teams took place on small-town ballfields and yielded little revenue. The players called the big Sunday doubleheaders in major league parks "gettin' out of the hole" days, when the teams hoped to make enough money to meet the payroll for the week. Many a time they raced dark rain clouds to the park, fidgeting in their seats, determined to play four and a half innings before the downpour so the game would be official and they would not have to refund the ticket money.

When the players stayed in a hotel, they often had to put newspaper between the mattress and the sheet to fend off the bedbugs; some hotels were so infested with roaches that the players slept with the lights on. They were not allowed to use the showers in the big league parks, so they would rent three rooms in a YMCA, where the whole team showered and changed uniforms before climbing back into the bus.

On the road, the players stopped at roadside diners. Even in the North they could not always get served, so they kept a supply of bread and cold cuts for midnight snacks. Needless to say, their diet was often irregular. One player recalled pitching a game one day on a hot dog, a Coke, and a lemon meringue pie.

While white major leaguers traveled by train, Negro leaguers had to make do with buses, often sleeping in their seats as they rode from city to city.

Light-skinned players got the assignment of going into restaurants to order take-out food. One night, when a dark-skinned Grays player suddenly awoke from a nap and ran in to order an extra hamburger, the waitress ordered him out, then took another look at the first man. "Are you with them?" she demanded, noticing the bus parked outside. For the sake of their empty stomachs, both men tried to deny knowing one another, but the waitress threatened to call the police and made them leave without their food. Most of the players found the incident funny, though one recalled, "Josh was so mad for messin' up the eatin' deal."

Despite their hardships, the Negro leaguers knew how to have fun. The Grays liked to sing barbershop harmony, imitating the Inkspots, a popular radio quartet. They often put themselves to sleep with their own music and the drone of the bus engine. Gibson in particular was always full of play. One of his pet

Jobless men line up at a Pittsburgh employment office during the depths of the Great Depression. Though the Negro leaguers of the 1930s endured a grueling schedule, they were glad to be making a living during the economic crisis gripping the nation.

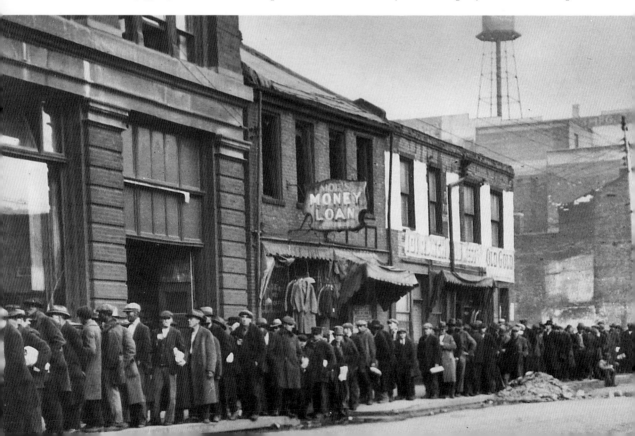

tricks was to wait until the bus entered a tunnel, then shout at the top of his voice. The echoes magnified the sound so much that sleeping players awoke with a start, while Gibson laughed with delight.

Essentially, the players took a hardheaded view of the world and made the best of their lot. "It was better than washing windows," Ted Page said. With so many Americans out of work, the Negro leaguers were glad to be making a living. Present-day fans, accustomed to the presence of black stars in most of the major sports, might wonder why the Negro leaguers did not demand the right to play in the majors. There was no law against it, just an unwritten rule that had never been broken since 1887. But in 1931, it was no easy matter for African Americans to challenge the status quo. Lynchings took place routinely in the South, and unofficial segregation was the rule in the North. "We thought the way things were was the way things were always going to be," said Buck Leonard, who later played with Gibson on the Grays. In 1931, a black player in the white majors was as hard to imagine as a man walking on the moon.

For this reason, the majority of baseball fans never got to see some of the nation's greatest players. Included among them was the most famous black pitcher in the world—Leroy "Satchel" Paige. On August 18, 1931, when the Grays played the Pittsburgh Crawfords, the professional incarnation of Gibson's semipro team, Gibson himself got his first look at Paige. For the next 15 years the careers of Gibson and Paige would be intertwined, and they would be the two most renowned black players in America until the advent of Jackie Robinson.

Seven years older than Gibson, Paige had been born in Mobile, Alabama, which was also the birthplace of Hank Aaron. He got his nickname as a boy when he earned money by carrying satchels at the train station. Tall and lean, Paige became one of the

Leroy "Satchel" Paige, who broke in with the Birmingham Black Barons in 1927, was one of the greatest pitchers in baseball history. In addition to a blazing fastball, Paige had nearly perfect control: "I could nip frosting off a cake," he once remarked.

hardest throwers in baseball history and may have had the best control of any pitcher who ever lived. He called his fastball his "be ball," because, he said, "it be where I want it to be." He warmed up by throwing the ball over a chewing gum wrapper instead of home plate. Some black batters said they could not even see his fastball. One batter once protested a strike call, saying, "That last one sounded a little low, didn't it, ump?"

Paige broke into the Negro leagues with the Birmingham Black Barons in 1927 and helped pitch them to the pennant. In 1931, however, he was having an off year; he won five league games and lost five. But win or lose, he always had a flair for publicity and was always saying and doing funny things.

In the historic first meeting between Gibson and Paige, the great pitcher did not start the game but was summoned from the bullpen in the fourth inning after the Grays scored five runs. He shut out the Homestead squad the rest of the way, and the Crawfords rallied to win the game. Gibson failed to get a hit. Before he had a chance for revenge, he and Paige were teammates. 🍂

4

THE CRAWFORDS

I N THE SPRING of 1932, Gibson and most of the other Grays, tempted by an offer of an extra $100 a month apiece, jumped to the Crawfords. Gibson and Paige formed what may have been the greatest battery in baseball history. They anchored what some authorities consider the greatest dynasty in blackball history, the Pittsburgh Crawfords of 1932–36. The Crawfords manager was Oscar Charleston, and the team also featured Judy Johnson and Cool Papa Bell. Along with Gibson and Paige, all are enshrined in the Baseball Hall of Fame.

The owner of the Crawfords was the flamboyant, cigar-chomping Gus Greenlee, the head of the numbers racket in Pittsburgh. Greenlee's business flourished despite the depression, as even the poorest people would often scrape up a penny or a nickel to play a number from 1 to 1,000, hoping for a big payoff. Though Greenlee lived on the wrong side of the law, he genuinely loved his ballplayers and the boxers he promoted, including John Henry Lewis, the eventual light-heavyweight champion of the world. In his own way, Greenlee was good for the game of baseball.

Gibson's career with the Crawfords got off to a difficult start. On the bus to spring training, Gibson was stricken by appendicitis and was rushed to a hospital. But he made a fast recovery from surgery and returned to the lineup within two weeks. How-

The Pittsburgh Crawfords of 1932 included (left to right) manager Oscar Charleston, Josh Gibson, Ted Page, and Judy Johnson. Many experts consider the 1932–36 Crawfords the greatest dynasty in Negro league history.

ever, he was moved to left field to make room for Bill Perkins, Paige's favorite catcher.

Greenlee was a shrewd showman. He often ran advertisements claiming that Gibson would hit a home run in an upcoming game and that Paige would strike out the first three batters he faced. Wisely, he did this only when the Crawfords played semipro clubs; nobody could make such a guarantee against the other black pro teams. To attract fans, the owner built a new stadium, Greenlee Field, that featured a brick grandstand covered by an awning. Paige pitched the opening game at Greenlee Field, facing the New York Black Yankees, owned by Bill "Bojangles" Robinson, the great tap dancer and movie actor.

The game was a memorable one, as Paige locked up in a duel with Jesse "Mountain" Hubbard, who took a 1–0 lead into the ninth. In the bottom of the ninth, Gibson came up with two men out. While the fans roared, Gibson's mother called him over to her box, planted a kiss on him, and told him to hit one out of the park.

With a count of one ball and two strikes, Gibson drove a screamer to deepest center, about 460 feet from the plate. Yankees center fielder Clint Thomas, nicknamed "Hawk" (and later "the black Joe DiMaggio"), turned his back and sprinted toward the fence. "Can you get it, Hawk? Can you get it, Hawk?" the other outfielders screamed. Thomas hit the fence with his right hand, turned, and stuck his glove hand up—the ball dropped into it for the final out. On July 10, Satchel got his revenge, hurling a no-hitter against the same Black Yankees. Gibson helped out with two hits.

Paige had one of the best years of his career in 1932, winning 14 games in the short Negro league season to lead all pitchers. He also had the most strikeouts, though he also led the league in losses, with eight.

From Gibson's point of view, Greenlee Field was a slight improvement over Forbes Field, though it was still a challenge for a right-handed hitter. The left-field foul line was about 350 feet from home, and the field sloped upward in that area, adding to the height of the wall. Even so, Gibson smacked 7 homers in 46 games to lead the league. His average dropped to .286, but he also slugged a league-best 5 triples.

That fall, the Crawfords hooked up for a seven-game series against a team of white all-stars piloted by Casey Stengel, later one of baseball's most successful managers. The Craws won the series, 5 games to 2. Only four box scores have been found, and they indicate that Gibson got 7 hits in 17 at-bats for a batting average of .412. Four of his hits came in a single game, in which Paige struck out 15 batters en route to a 10–2 victory.

One of Stengel's pitchers, Fred Frankhouse of the Boston Braves, remembered that Gibson could throw out runners without getting up from his crouch. Frankhouse told Charleston he thought the time would come when blacks would get into the white major leagues.

For the moment, their main concern was survival. The year 1933 marked the depth of the depression. One out of four Americans was out of work. Greenlee told the Crawfords, "There will be no big salaries for any of the players this year." He set about to re-form a league with six teams: the Crawfords, the Chicago American Giants, the Baltimore Black Sox, the Nashville Elite Giants, the Detroit Stars, and the Columbus Blue Birds. Some of the teams changed in the next three years, but the league continued until 1937, when it split up into two leagues again: the Negro National League in the East and the Negro American League in the West. Greenlee's six-team league played a split schedule of 60 games, 30 in the first half of the season and 30 in the second.

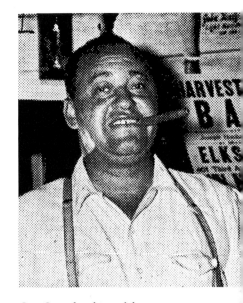

Gus Greenlee, king of the Pittsburgh numbers racket, organized the Crawfords in 1931. The team's name was borrowed from the local semipro squad that Gibson has played on as a teenager.

George "Mule" Suttles, a burly Alabaman who played first base and outfield for a variety of Negro league teams between 1918 and 1943, rivaled Gibson as a power hitter but could not match the great catcher's all-around batting skills.

That summer, Gibson hit another mighty home run, one of the longest he ever swatted. It came in the grimy little coal-mining town of Monessen, Pennsylvania, in a game against the Chicago American Giants. People in Monessen still point to the spot where the ball came down in front of a watchman's shack, after clearing the fence and an apple tree. The mayor of the town was so impressed that he had a measurement made. The distance was 512 feet.

Larry Brown, who had been the catcher when Gibson hit his famous Yankee Stadium homer in 1930, was behind the plate for this legendary blast as well. After the inning was over, Brown stormed into the dugout and slammed his mask against the wall. "What did you call for, Larry?" the Chicago players asked.

"A fastball," Brown snarled.

"Why didn't you call for a curve?" someone asked.

"If I'd knowed he was gonna hit the fastball," Larry snapped, "I *woulda* called for a curve!"

Cool Papa Bell kept track of Gibson's home runs during the season, comparing him to the powerful Mule Suttles, Bell's old teammate at St. Louis. According to his calculations, Gibson hit 72 balls out of the park, which topped Suttles's best total of 69.

The two musclemen went head-to-head in September when Gus Greenlee organized a black all-star game, called the East-West Game. That summer, the major leagues held their first All-Star Game, and Babe Ruth, enjoying his last productive season, had hit a two-run homer for the American League. Like the major league All-Star Game, the East-West Game was played in Chicago's Comiskey Park. In the game, Gibson hit two singles, but Suttles topped him with a powerful home run that sailed through the open space between the left-field upper deck and the roof, landing in the street outside.

For the season, Gibson batted .362, with 6 home runs, but the Craws lost the pennant to Chicago by one game, mainly because of Satchel Paige's poor performance. He had one of the worst years of his career, winning only 5 and losing 7, and he deserted the team before the season was over to go out to North Dakota and pitch with a white semipro team. That winter, Paige sailed to Venezuela to pick up some extra money playing winter ball, while Gibson caught a boat to the Caribbean to play in the Cuban winter league.

Back in Pittsburgh in 1934, Greenlee, a genius at promoting his stars to the public, advertised Satch and Josh in every town they went to. Some of the other players resented it. But outfielder Ted Page defended Gibson. "Of course he deserved all the attention," Ted said. "He was a terrific hitter."

Paige, in his autobiography, *Don't Look Back,* was equally blunt. "Gus knew I was pulling in the big crowds," he wrote. "Those other fellows ate that lean meat because I pulled like that. If it wasn't for me, they'd have been eating side meat, that's what."

In 1934, Paige reeled off four straight shutouts. In one of the games he allowed only one hit, and he finished the streak in grand style. On July 4, he hurled a no-hitter against the Grays, striking out 17. "He threw *fire*," marveled the Grays' rookie first baseman, Buck Leonard. Paige's fastball had so much movement on it that Leonard kept calling for the ball and asking the umpire to take a look at it. "You may as well throw them all out," Paige called with a laugh, "because they're all gonna jump like that." He recalled that one fan "kept shooting off firecrackers every time I got a man out." Meanwhile, Gibson drove Bell home in the first inning to give Paige the only run he needed.

Gibson also called the pitches during Paige's

no-hitter. It was the second masterpiece he had caught, starting with the great Smoky Joe Williams– Chet Brewer duel back in 1930. Gibson's critics always contended that although he had a fine throwing arm he could not field his position. However, they overlook the fact that Gibson was an excellent handler of pitchers, which is perhaps the most valuable skill any catcher can have.

That night after Paige's classic, the Crawfords boarded their bus for the all-night ride to Chicago to meet the American Giants, winners of the first-half pennant. Pitching with two days rest, Paige came up against Willie "Sugar" Cornelius, who turned the tables and pitched a no-hitter of his own. But Satchel matched him in scoreless innings right into the 10th.

A Crawfords game in progress at Pittsburgh's Greenlee Field. Due to their owner's lavish bankroll, the Crawfords were one of the few black teams to have their own home ballpark.

Then, with two out, Judy Johnson lifted a routine fly to center, but the Chicago center fielder got a slow jump on the ball, which fell in front of him for the Craws' first hit. Cornelius then threw a curve to Gibson that the pitcher claimed was three feet outside. Nevertheless, Gibson threw his bat at the ball and singled to right field. The next man also singled, and the Crawfords won the game.

Throughout the summer of 1934, a skinny left-handed rookie for the Philadelphia Stars, Stewart "Slim" Jones, was having one of the greatest seasons in blackball annals. Jones looked—and pitched—like a left-handed Paige. Some players who faced him said that Jones was even faster than Lefty Grove of the old Philadelphia Athletics or Sandy Koufax, the great Dodgers left-hander of the 1960s. Even Paige admitted that Jones was the fastest pitcher he had ever seen, better than Dizzy Dean of the Cardinals or Bob Feller of the Indians.

In the first meeting between the Crawfords and the Stars, Gibson hit a homer against Jones, although Slim beat Satchel anyway, 10–5. Beginning with that victory, Jones reeled off 18 straight wins, including 2 over the Crawfords. (The white major league record was 20 straight in one season, set by Rube Marquard of the New York Giants in 1912.) Gibson, however, had no trouble hitting Jones. In their fourth and final encounter, Gibson smashed five hits—a single, double, triple, and two home runs—as the Crawfords mauled the lefty, 8–2, breaking his string of victories. In four games, Gibson's batting average against Jones was .529.

In the East-West Game, the two antagonists were on the same side. Gibson was behind the plate as Jones pitched the first three innings, striking out four. Gibson helped by rifling a throw to third in the first inning to cut down one runner attempting to steal. Gibson threw out another runner later in the game and put the tag on big Mule Suttles, who came barreling into the plate on a sacrifice fly as the crowd roared with excitement. At bat, Gibson smacked a double and single against Ted Trent and Chet Brewer. Paige entered the game in the seventh inning, when it was still scoreless. He shut out the West stars the rest of the way, and Bell scored the game's only run when he walked, stole second, and scored on a broken-bat infield hit.

By season's end, Paige had perhaps the best year of his life, 13-3, with a total run average of 1.99. (Negro league box scores did not keep track of earned and unearned runs, so it is not possible to compute earned run averages.) However, Jones was even better, finishing the year with a 22-3 mark as Philadelphia won the second-half pennant. Gibson hit .315 for the season but almost doubled his home run output to 11. The next two men, Suttles and Turkey Stearnes of Chicago, hit only 6 apiece.

After the regular season, the two great hurlers, Jones and Paige, were called out to meet each other face-to-face in Yankee Stadium. It was one of the greatest pitching duels of all time. Jones finally held Gibson hitless and had a no-hitter for six innings until Charleston broke it up with a single. Paige gave up six hits, but he struck out 16 men through eight innings while some sensational fielding behind him held the score to 1–1.

In the last of the ninth, with one out, the Stars' Jud Wilson beat out a slow roller and chugged all the way to third on a wild throw. As the autumn shadows grew deeper, Paige whiffed pinch-hitter Webster McDonald for strikeout number 17. Another pinch-hitter, Chester Brooks, also went down swinging, and the game ended in a 1–1 tie. At the time, the combined total of 33 strikeouts set a world record for a nine-inning game.

After the season, Gibson and Paige went out on

Satchel Paige warming up before a Negro league game at New York's Yankee Stadium. During the 1930s, Paige and Gibson were the leading gate attractions in black baseball: whenever they barnstormed against white major leaguers, they proved that they were among the best ballplayers in the nation.

the barnstorming circuit, where they faced a number of white stars, including the St. Louis Cardinals aces Dizzy and Paul Dean. The Deans were backed by a semipro cast and seemed to be just fooling around to pick up some much-needed depression money instead of playing seriously to win.

Paige won the first game with 13 strikeouts and no hits in 6 innings in Cleveland. In Philadelphia, Gibson drilled three hits, including a triple, against Dizzy. Finally, in York, Pennsylvania, Gibson slammed a home run in the first and another in the third, and Dean took himself out of the game as the crowd booed. As Diz trotted past the Crawfords dugout, he grinned and mopped his brow, saying, "Josh, I wish you and Satch played with me 'n' Paul on the Cardinals. We'd win the pennant by July 4th and go fishin' the rest of the year."

Gibson showed his combative nature when the tour moved to Pittsburgh and a bench-clearing brawl broke out on the field.

Ted Page ran in from the outfield to get into it and remembered:

> Josh and George Susce [catcher for the Deans] were rolling around, and Gibson had Susce down in the corner between the fence and the dugout. Dizzy Dean and I were trying to pull Josh out of there, because he was strong, and there was no telling what he might do to any man, when he got him in a crack like that. But heck, he threw Dean from here to there, just shook him and shoved him out of the way, and never let go of Susce with the other hand. I can see Josh today, when that was over. He was kind of scratched up and had lost his cap in the scuffle, but he had a big grin on his face, you know, one of those satisfied grins, like, "Well, this was a good one."

Gibson would never pass up a fight, Page said, but he would not start one either: "Life was a beautiful thing for him. He enjoyed it. Big and strong, able to take part in any kind of ruckus that came along, or play baseball. He was happy with life."

Even Oscar Charleston, one of the most notorious fighters in Negro league annals, was afraid of Gibson. Once Charleston threatened to punch Cool Papa Bell until Gibson stepped in and grabbed the manager in a headlock. After that, Bell told baseball historian Jim Bankes, "Charleston stayed clear of him."

Another time, in the South, a fan threw a chair onto the field, just missing Bell. Gibson charged into the stands. That was not a smart thing to do, Bell said, but he recalled that "Josh looked so big and powerful" that nobody made a move against him. ✦

5

"THOSE ARE BIG LEAGUERS"

❦

DURING THE WINTER of 1934–35, Gibson played winter ball in Puerto Rico, where he unloaded another of his mammoth blows. Even though a strong wind was blowing in, the ball traveled more than 500 feet. Johnny Mize, the slugging star of the St. Louis Cardinals, witnessed Gibson's feat. "Josh was at second base when the ball cleared the fence," Mize said, "and he jumped straight up in the air, [because he had] figured no one was going to hit one that far."

Gibson also worked on his fielding over the winter. Buck Leonard said Gibson worked out by the hour on catching pop fouls, running the bases, and other fundamental skills. "After two or three winters of that, he could catch anything," Leonard said.

At spring training in Florida, the great white pitcher Walter Johnson watched Gibson catch. "That boy is worth $200,000 of anybody's money," he exclaimed. "He can do everything. Hits the ball a mile. And he catches so easy he might as well be in a rocking chair. Throws like a rifle. Bill Dickey [of the Yankees] isn't as good a catcher. Too bad this Gibson is a colored fellow."

President Franklin D. Roosevelt throws out the ceremonial first ball of the 1936 baseball season on April 14, at Griffith Stadium in Washington, D.C. Though baseball was enjoying unprecedented popularity during the 1930s, African Americans were still excluded from the major leagues.

A few years later, 15-year-old Roy Campanella, who became a Negro league star and then a Hall of Fame catcher for the Brooklyn Dodgers, saw Gibson play for the first time. As Campanella later wrote, he was even more impressed with Gibson's catching than his hitting. According to Campanella, Gibson had "a huge chest, tremendous shoulders, and the biggest arms I've ever seen. With all that weight, he moved around behind the plate with such effortless grace that everything he did looked easy."

New York Giants Hall of Famer Carl Hubbell called Gibson "one of the fastest big men I've ever seen," and Negro leaguer Gene Benson testified that Gibson was an aggressive and intimidating baserunner. "He came in with spikes high," said Benson, who once saw Gibson almost cut an infielder's uniform off with his spikes.

With Gibson now a complete player, the Crawfords were looking forward to perhaps their greatest year, only to have Paige jump the team to play in North Dakota again. But two veteran pitchers, Roosevelt Davis and Leroy Matlock, filled the void. Davis was a wily "cut-ball" artist, and the left-handed Matlock, while not overpowering, had almost perfect control. In 1931, Matlock had beaten a team led by three white Hall of Famers—Bill Terry, Paul Waner, and Lloyd Waner—by a score of 18–1. "I couldn't hit him with a paddle," complained Ted Page. "He gave me a fit," Buck Leonard agreed. With Davis and Matlock leading the way, the Crawfords ran away with the first-half pennant. Davis finished with a 15-4 record, more victories than Paige ever had in a season. Matlock did even better. He chalked up a perfect 18-0 record, tying Slim Jones's single-season feat of the year before. Gibson batted .333 and led in home runs again.

After the Negro league season, the Crawfords traveled to Denver, Colorado, for the nationwide semipro tournament sponsored by the *Denver Post*. The Craws won the tournament easily. "Those are big leaguers," one of the white players protested. "They're niggers, but they're big leaguers."

The Craws returned to Chicago for the East-West Game, and Gibson had a great day, hitting two doubles and two singles in five at-bats. One of the doubles traveled 436 feet to the center-field wall. Meanwhile, Gibson's rival, Mule Suttles, was having a frustrating time. He had three bases on balls and only one official at-bat, a strikeout. But in the 11th inning he drove a ball high into the upper deck in right field, winning the game and stealing Gibson's glory.

While the Craws had been in Denver, the New York Cubans had won the second-half pennant, and the two clubs met in a playoff showdown. The Cubans won the first two games, including a 4–0 win

Pitcher Willie Foster of the Chicago American Giants receives an award prior to the 1934 East-West Game at Chicago's Comiskey Park. The annual East-West Game was organized by the Negro leagues in response to the white major leagues' All-Star Game, staged for the first time in 1933.

over Davis. Charleston rushed Matlock in to pitch Game 3 and try to stop the slide. Matlock's mound opponent was Schoolboy Johnny Taylor, a young right-hander who had a 7-3 record for the year. In the first inning, Gibson came up with a man on base and smashed a 3-2 pitch off the center-field wall for a triple to give Matlock a one-run lead. That was all Matlock needed, as he won 3–0, his 19th victory in a row.

The immortal Cuban outfielder-pitcher, Martin Dihigo, who was the New Yorkers' manager, put himself in to pitch Game 4 and gave the Cubans a 3–1 lead in the series. The Craws would have to sweep all three remaining games or be eliminated. Davis won the fifth game to keep the Crawfords alive, and Matlock started the sixth game against Taylor. The Cubans were ahead 5–2 in the eighth, and Cubans business manager Frank Forbes was already under the stands counting out the winners' share of the money, when Dihigo suddenly pulled Taylor out for no apparent reason and put himself in to pitch. A few moments later, Forbes heard the crowd roar as Charleston slugged a three-run homer to tie the game. Then, with a man on second, Judy Johnson drilled a 3-2 pitch past the first baseman to win the game as Forbes threw the thick wad of bills across the room in disgust. The Crawfords had tied the series, and Matlock had won his 20th game in a row.

It all came down to the seventh game against Cubans lefty Luis Tiant, Sr., whose son Luis junior later won 223 games with the Indians, Red Sox, and Yankees. The senior Tiant, with a 7-4 record that year, was mainly a "junkball" pitcher relying on slow curves, change-ups, and the like. He also had a brilliant pick-off move: some old-timers claim that one time he threw to first base and the batter swung at the ball.

Cuban-born Martín Dihigo (shown here during the latter part of his career) was a multitalented star who both pitched and played the outfield, often in the same game. In the 1935 East-West Game, for example, he started in center field for the East team and finished the game as the losing pitcher.

With Tiant tantalizing them, the Craws fell behind 7–5 in Game 7. Then Gibson homered over the center-field wall, and Charleston followed with another round-tripper to tie the game. Bell singled and scored on an error, and the Crawfords were champs. They had no one left to beat but the whites.

This time they found that they were playing under a different set of rules. With Bell on second base during a barnstorming game at Yankee Stadium, Gibson came up to bat against Dizzy Dean. Dean turned and signaled his center fielder, Jimmy Ripple

Dizzy Dean, a Hall of Fame pitcher for the St. Louis Cardinals, often barnstormed against black stars during the winter months. Dean once told Gibson, "Josh, if you and Satch played with Paul [Dean] 'n' me on the Cardinals, we'd win the pennant by July 4th and go fishin' the rest of the year."

of the Cincinnati Reds, to move back. Ripple backed up a step or two. Dean waved him back farther, and Ripple took two more steps toward the fence. Once again, Dean waved him back. At last, apparently satisfied, he turned and delivered the ball. Gibson drilled the pitch to deep center field, 460 feet away, where Ripple was waiting.

Bell tagged up when Ripple made the catch, raced around third base, and slid into home well ahead of the ball. The umpire jerked a thumb and yelled, "Out!"

"Out?" the usually mild-mannered Bell protested.

"Yes," said the ump. "You don't *do* that against big leaguers."

In 1936, Greenlee meekly welcomed back Paige, who reclaimed his place as king of the Crawfords. Matlock won his first two games for a string of 22 straight victories before he finally lost a game. (Two years later, the New York Giants' Carl Hubbell would win 24 in a row over two seasons, but he suffered a World Series loss in between.) Matlock split his next two decisions before leaving the team for reasons unknown. Davis also could not repeat his 1935 heroics. Luckily for the Craws, Paige resumed his old form with a 10-3 record to top the league in victories. No one else on the team could win more than three games.

Gibson had a magnificent year. In only 23 league games, he crashed 11 home runs, a pace that would have given him 81 in a regulation modern season. He beat out Suttles and Dihigo for the league lead by one. Some reports claim that in 170 total games that year, league and semipro, Gibson blasted 84 homers and batted .360. No one else on the Craws hit over .300.

At this point, the Craws were virtually a two-man team: Josh and Satch. They finished third in the first half over Baltimore and won the second half. There was no playoff, however. Instead, the two Negro league champs joined forces in the *Denver Post* tourney, sweeping all seven games.

That winter, Greenlee took his club to Mexico. Their hosts rushed them onto the field against a touring big league squad without giving them a chance to get used to the higher altitude, which makes players tire more quickly until they adjust. The game pitted Gibson against Jimmie Foxx, America's best white long-ball hitter, who had hit 41 homers that year and 58 four years earlier.

With two out in the ninth, the Craws were leading 6–4 when Foxx came to bat with a man on base. With a count of 2-2, Roosevelt Davis fired one

Gibson and James "Cool Papa" Bell in the uniform of the Trujillo Dragones (Dragons) during the winter of 1936–37. The Negro league stars often made good money in the off-season by playing in Cuba, Puerto Rico, and the Dominican Republic.

over the plate, but the umpire called it ball three. Foxx then lashed the next pitch over the fence to tie the game. The teams battled into the 11th, when the whites loaded the bases with two out and Foxx up again. This time Foxx grounded out, and the umpire called the game. "The sun's in the sky and they call the game!" Bell exclaimed in disgust. After the game the two teams met for dinner, and Foxx confessed that that third pitch had been a strike. "But I wasn't going to argue," he smiled, picking up the dinner check.

The next day, future Hall of Famer Ted Lyons shut the Crawfords out 11–0 as Gibson went 0-for-4. Finally, Jack Knott of the St. Louis Browns beat them 7–2, though Gibson got two hits.

That was the last hurrah for the Crawfords, perhaps the greatest black team of all time. They never played together again. Over the winter, Greenlee was having political troubles. New elections had swept a reform government into office in Pittsburgh, and the police no longer telephoned before they raided his numbers operation. As Greenlee's numbers income dried up, he could no longer meet the salary demands of his baseball stars. The first sign of trouble was the announcement that players would have to pay their own expenses to spring training.

Meanwhile, Rafael Trujillo, the dictator of the Dominican Republic and owner of the Dragones (Dragons) baseball team, sent his agents to New Orleans with $30,000 in cash for Paige. They told him to pick eight other players at $3,000 each and keep the change. The first two men Satchel thought of were Gibson and Bell.

When the Negro leaguers arrived in the Dominican Republic, the Dragones were not doing too well. Gibson also got off to a slow start, coming to bat 12 times without a hit. The rival Eastern Stars club had also brought down some top black players from the

United States, including Chet Brewer, who tossed a no-hitter in one game to beat Paige.

Trujillo was displeased. Troops with weapons slung over their shoulders patrolled the games. "El President doesn't lose," Paige and Gibson were warned, and they got the message. The hits began flying off Gibson's bat until he was hitting .453, 100 points better than runner-up Dihigo. Strangely, Gibson hit only two homers. Paige also began winning and went into the championship game against the Stars with a 7-2 record.

The night before the game, Brewer strolled over to the Dragones' hotel to find the team gone. "Where is everyone?" he asked a kid. "*En el carcel*," the boy answered, jerking his thumb toward the jail. Trujillo had ordered the players locked up for the night to make sure that they would be in good shape for the big game.

By game time, troops were lined up along each foul line—"like firing squads," Paige nervously noted. "They don't kill people over baseball?" Bell asked. "Down here they do," came the answer. Paige said he never pitched harder in his life, winning the game 4–3 and hurrying gratefully out of town.

That dramatic afternoon marked the last time Josh and Satch ever played together. The U.S. season was only half over when they got back, and Gibson's old boss, Cum Posey of the Grays, offered to buy him and Judy Johnson ("the Punch and Judy show") from the financially strapped Greenlee. The transaction, at a price of $25,000, was hailed as "the biggest player deal in the history of Negro baseball." ❧

6

NEW LIFE

❦

ACCORDING TO BUCK LEONARD, Gibson "put new life into everybody" when he joined the Grays. For three years, Leonard had been carrying the team alone as Posey struggled to rebuild after losing his greatest stars to the Crawfords. In 1936, the Grays had finished last. But for most of the next decade, Gibson and Leonard would become the most powerful home run duo since the Yankees' Lou Gehrig and Babe Ruth. There would not be another pair to match the two black sluggers until Hank Aaron and Eddie Mathews teamed up for the Milwaukee Braves in the late 1950s.

The change of teams put some new life into Gibson as well. With Leonard hitting behind him, pitchers had to give Gibson better pitches to hit. In the next decade, Gibson would run up some of the highest batting averages ever seen in the Negro leagues.

Gibson was not lucky in the choice of a home park, however. He had played the first seven years of his career in Forbes Field and Greenlee Field, two tough parks for a right-handed slugger. In 1937, Posey decided to split the Grays games between two different sites: half would be played in Forbes Field and half in Washington's Griffith Stadium. If Forbes Field was a difficult place to hit a home run, Griffith Stadium was even worse. The field measured 407 feet

Eluding the tag of Ted "Double Duty" Radcliffe, Gibson scores a run during the 1942 East-West Game at Comiskey Park. After returning to his original team, the Homestead Grays, in 1937, Gibson enjoyed some of his finest seasons.

down the left-field line and 430 feet in dead center, where a 30-foot high wall loomed above the field. If Babe Ruth had played in Washington, instead of in Yankee Stadium, he might have hit closer to 400 home runs in his career instead of 714.

Despite the obstacles, Gibson hit two of the longest homers of his career during the summer of 1937. The first came in East Orange, New Jersey, against a semipro club. "I hit it over the left-field fence and over a two-story station outside the park," he said.

Gibson hit the second blast in Yankee Stadium, and it was almost as long as his famous 1930 clout that hit the back wall of the bullpen. Some eyewitnesses claimed that the ball went over the roof and came down in the bullpen, but this is unlikely, given the height of the roof and the fact that Gibson hit mostly line drives rather than high flies. Bill Yancey, playing shortstop for the New York Black Yankees, called Gibson's shot the "quickest" home run he had ever seen. "It was out of the park before the outfielders could turn their heads to look at it." Outfielder Clint Thomas watched in amazement as the ball hit the bullpen sod and bounced up into the bleachers. "Jesus Christ!" he exclaimed to left-fielder Fats Jenkins. "I ain't *never* seen a ball hit like that before!" "Neither have I, Roomie," Fats gasped.

Gibson got into only 12 league games after joining the Grays, but he batted an even .500 while slugging 7 home runs. At that pace, he would have hit 92 home runs in a full big league season. Mule Suttles, playing twice as many games, beat him out in homers, with 12, but Gibson hit more triples (4) than anyone in the league. His slugging average (total bases divided by at-bats) was 1.190, which means he averaged more than one base every time he came to bat. Babe Ruth's best mark was 0.847 in 1920.

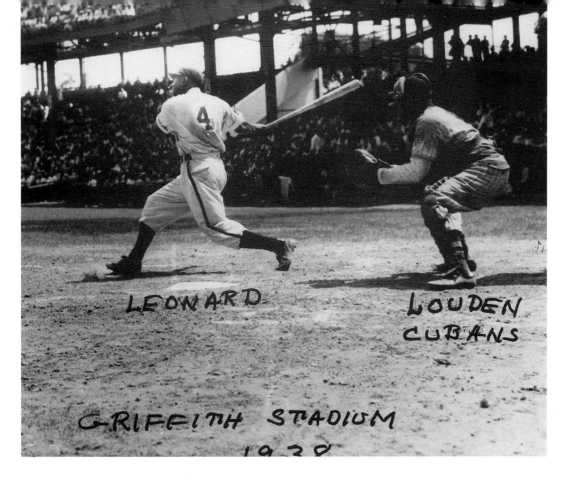

The Grays charged from last place in 1936 to the pennant in 1937, making them the first team to accomplish the feat in modern times, 55 years before the Minnesota Twins and Atlanta Braves did it in 1991. It was the first of nine straight pennants the Grays would win. No professional team in any sport in any era has ever topped that, although the Tokyo Giants of Sadaharu Oh later tied the mark.

There was no black World Series in 1937, but the Grays and Newark Eagles did combine to play a game against the Western champion Kansas City Monarchs. The Monarchs' star slugger was Willard "Home Run" Brown. For the rest of Gibson's life he would duel Brown for the title of America's most powerful black hitter. In the championship game, Brown and Turkey Stearnes homered for Kansas City, and Gib-

Buck Leonard (4), a slugging first baseman and future Hall of Famer, was the Grays' best player when Gibson rejoined the team. Together, Gibson and Leonard provided a one-two punch that compared with the legendary New York Yankees duo, Babe Ruth and Lou Gehrig.

son homered and tripled for the Easterners, who won the free-swinging contest, 14–12.

Then Gibson went barnstorming against a squad of white major leaguers, including Leo Durocher of the Cardinals, who was later to manage a number of major league teams. No box scores have been found for the games, but Gibson reportedly hit three home runs as his team won the series, 5 games to 3. The hard-bitten Durocher was awed. He later told a reporter, "Everything they said about Gibson was true, and then some. He caught hold of one of [Pittsburgh right-hander] Jim Weaver's fast ones, and I'll bet you it's still sailing."

After a winter in Cuba, Gibson in 1938 again demonstrated his skill as a handler of pitchers, teaming up with right-hander Ray Brown to form the best battery in the Negro leagues. The temperamental Brown, who was married to Cum Posey's daughter, had a dancing knuckleball to complement his fastball and curve. He could also hit and usually played the outfield when not pitching. Sometimes he would pitch the first game of a double-header and come in to relieve in the second game.

Grays manager Vic Harris found Brown hard to manage, and his being the owner's son-in-law did not

The talented and temperamental Ray Brown was the Grays' top pitcher during the Gibson-Leonard era. During the 1940 season, which spanned only 50 games, Brown chalked up 24 wins against a mere 4 losses.

make Brown any easier to get along with. So Harris was happy to have Gibson take charge. When Gibson hollered to Harris, who also played left field, "How about walking this man?" Harris just hollered back, "Suit yourself." Harris later said, "I just let Gibson use his own judgment. There was no one easier to handle than Josh Gibson."

Gibson had an off-year as a slugger, with only four home runs, compared to nine by Suttles, the league leader, who played in the tiny Newark bandbox. Though his power output was down, Gibson batted .350. But under Gibson's guidance, Brown posted a perfect 7-0 record, as the Grays won their second pennant in a row.

That summer there was a flurry of speculation that the white big leagues might open their doors to blacks. The sports editor of the *Pittsburgh Courier* wired Pie Traynor, manager of the third-place Pirates:

KNOW YOUR CLUB NEEDS PLAYERS. HAVE ANSWERS TO YOUR PRAYERS RIGHT HERE IN PITTSBURGH. JOSH GIBSON CATCHER, 1B B. LEONARD, AND RAY BROWN PITCHER OF HOMESTEAD GRAYS, AND S. PAIGE, PITCHER, AND COOL PAPA BELL OF PITTSBURGH CRAWFORDS ALL AVAILABLE AT REASONABLE FIGURES. WOULD MAKE PIRATES FORMIDABLE PENNANT CONTENDERS. WHAT IS YOUR ATTITUDE? WIRE ANSWER.

Traynor's answer was eloquent: He did not reply. By September, the Pirates were locked in a pennant race with the Chicago Cubs and New York Giants, and *New York Daily News* columnist Jimmy Powers demanded to know why the Giants did not pick up Gibson, Leonard, Brown, and Newark third baseman Ray Dandridge. If they did, he wrote, they could win the pennant. Like the Pirates, the Giants also passed up a chance to obtain the black stars, and the Cubs finished in first place.

When National League president Ford Frick was asked why baseball did not integrate, he pointed to public opinion and the problem of traveling in the South. "Baseball is biding its time and waiting for the social change, which is inevitable," Frick said. "I think that in the near future, people will be willing to accept a Negro ballplayer just as they have the Negro boxer and college athlete. Times are changing."

In the fall of 1938, the Grays went to Cuba and were shocked to lose four out of six to the strong Cuban players. Gibson stayed on for the regular winter season. Despite the huge Cuban ballparks, he set a Cuban home run record with 11 round-trippers, wiping out Mule Suttles's previous record of 7.

Back in the United States in 1939, Gibson had his greatest year at the plate, walloping homers at an unbelievable rate—17 in only 88 at-bats. At that rate, he would have hit 106 in a full major league season (550 at-bats). He also hit 2 triples and 2 doubles—only 8 of his 29 hits were singles, a remarkable figure for a batter posting a .330 average. Gibson's slugging average was .977.

One of Gibson's longest blows came in Beckley, West Virginia, in a game against the Baltimore Elite Giants. The park was at the base of a large hill, and Gibson smashed four home runs: one over the fence, one to the foot of the hill, one halfway up the hill, and the fourth—according to Roy Campanella, then a 17-year-old rookie with the Elite Giants—"clear over the hill." Leonard recalls watching a group of boys on top of the hill looking for the ball.

When the Grays played in Washington, Clark Griffith, owner of the Washington Senators, used to go down to the dugout during the games and sit beside Gibson. "Josh, you gonna hit a home run for me today?" he'd ask. "Well, I'll try, Mr Griffith," Gibson would always answer. One day, according to Eric

Roberts, Gibson hit one over the bleachers in Griffith Stadium. Only Mickey Mantle has done it since, a blow measured at 563 feet. Ric Roberts saw both drives: "Josh's was higher than Mantle's. Mantle's just got over. Gibson's went over with room to spare! Mr Griffith almost ate his cigar!"

Gibson's favorite park was New York's Polo Grounds, which was shaped like a race track or a football stadium. Center field was extremely deep, but it was only 279 feet to the left-field foul pole and only 257 to right, where Gibson loved to park outside curve balls. The deepest corners were in left-center and right-center, more than 500 feet away: they were so distant that the bullpens were located there, not behind the fence but right out on the playing field. Grays shortstop Sammy Bankhead said he saw Gibson blast one "upstairs, above the [left-field] bullpen, out of the park." An elevated train line ran outside the

The Polo Grounds, home of the New York Giants, was Gibson's favorite hitting venue. One of his most titanic shots carried over the roof in left-center field (arrow) and landed on the elevated subway tracks across the street from the ballpark.

park, and Leonard said a man came in with a ball, asking, "Who hit this ball onto the train track?"

As Gibson awed spectators and fellow players with his displays of power, he impressed others with his character. Roy Campanella always remained grateful to Gibson for his help. "I was a skinny little catcher away from home for the first time, and he was the great man of baseball," Campanella later wrote. The youngster had trouble making acccurate throws but, he recalled, Gibson "showed me how to set myself to improve my speed and accuracy, and when I had a bad day against the Grays, he'd come over to me in the locker room and try to give me a little confidence. 'It's just a matter of practice,' he'd tell me. 'You got the arm, that's the important thing. The rest is just practice, practice, practice.' "

Even though most of the Grays slumped at bat and on the pitching mound, Gibson carried the team to its third straight pennant in 1938. They won both halves of the split season.

Jacob Ruppert, co-owner of the New York Yankees, donated a cup to the winner of a special playoff among the top four teams in the East: the Grays, the New York Cubans, the Baltimore Elite Giants, and the Philadelphia Stars. The Grays beat the Stars, 4 games to 1, and the Elites upset the Cubans, 3 games to 2, setting up a showdown between the Grays and Baltimore.

The Elites had a great double-play combination in shortstop Tommy "Pee Wee" Butts and second baseman Sammy T. Hughes. Outfielder Wild Bill Wright, a former football running back, batted .402 and led the league in steals and triples. Campanella batted .237.

The spitball specialist Bill Byrd led the Baltimore pitchers with a 9-4 record. (During his career Byrd won 115 games in the Negro leagues, almost as many as Satchel Paige's 123.) Game 1 pitted Byrd against

Grays rookie Roy Partlow, who six years later would go with Jackie Robinson to the Dodgers farm team in Montreal. Byrd shut down Gibson without a hit, but Partlow pitched brilliantly, and the Grays won, 2–1.

The second game seesawed back and forth. Gibson's home run gave the Grays a 2–0 lead. But Wright's long triple sparked a rally that put Baltimore ahead 4–3 in the fourth. The Grays tied it in the fifth on a single, a walk to Gibson, and a single by Leonard. In the sixth, Gibson made an error that contributed to a 6–4 Baltimore lead. The Elites hung on for a 6–5 win, as Gibson went hitless after his first-inning homer.

In Game 3, young Campanella made two errors to let in a run, but the Elites tied it in the third on two errors by the Grays, and the game ended in a 1–1 tie. Game 4 turned into a duel between the rival catchers. Campanella doubled in two runs to give Baltimore a 2–0 lead. Gibson homered to get one run back, and Leonard's single made it 2–2. Gibson then singled in two runs, but Campanella answered back with a two-run homer. Finally, Campanella's two-run double capped a rally that put the game out of reach, 10–5. The Grays were now down 2 games to 1.

The teams moved to Yankee Stadium for the fifth game. Gibson smashed one to the 467-foot sign in left-center, but Wright galloped back and pulled it down. In the sixth, Wright stroked a double, and Campanella singled him home with the only run Baltimore would need. They won the game, 2–0, and took the playoff. No one realized it at the time, but the playoff marked the end of Gibson's carefree days.

7

ADVENTURES IN LATIN
AMERICA

Gibson (standing, fourth from right) poses with other members of the Santurce Cangrejeros (Crabbers) during the 1939–40 winter league season. In addition to being the team's catcher, Gibson was also the manager.

A S THE 1930s were coming to an end, Ted Page noticed a change in the once happy-go-lucky Gibson. "He began to realize that he was perhaps the greatest hitter in the world," Page recalled, "and yet he was deprived of a chance to make thirty, forty, fifty thousand, while Babe Ruth had pulled down eighty thousand. He realized that he was just as good as Ruth. He changed from the Josh I knew—an over-grown kid who did nothing but play ball, eat ice cream, or go to the movies. He changed to a man who was kind of bitter with somebody, or mad with somebody. He realized as he started to get older that his good days were behind him, and I feel certain that in his mind Josh realized that he was never going to make the big leagues, so who cares? He started to drink."

The drinking did not have any immediate effect on the great catcher's busy baseball life. Gibson and the Grays returned to Cuba in the autumn of 1939, and this time they swept their six games there. Then Gibson was off to Puerto Rico, where he had been offered a job managing the new Santurce club. The island provided the setting for a reunion between Gibson and Paige, who for almost three years had been nurturing a sore arm that almost ended his career. Puerto Rico was the first real test of Paige's ability to come back as a big-time pitcher.

BOTO LA
PELOTA
AYER

The legend on this photo of Gibson in a Puerto Rican newspaper reads HE LAUNCHED THE BALL YESTERDAY. *Gibson's celebrity in Puerto Rico was a welcome contrast to the prejudice he encountered at home, but the easy lifestyle he enjoyed on the island also led him into bad habits.*

Winter baseball in Puerto Rico was virtually as good as the stateside Negro leagues, as many black stars went south for the winter—just as many of the Latin stars journeyed north every summer. The biggest star on the island was a tall second baseman named Perucho Cepeda, who played with Paige on the Guayama team. (Perucho's son Orlando would hit 379 home runs with the Cardinals and other big league teams, but the dark-skinned Perucho could not gain entry to the major leagues, and he refused to play in the United States at all because of the segregation laws.) Many Puerto Rican fans consider Perucho Cepeda the island's greatest all-time player, better than his son and even superior to the Hall of Famer Roberto Clemente.

Gibson amazed the Puerto Ricans with his feats of strength. Once he spotted a heavy wooden ox cart stuck in a ditch, put his arm under the wheel, and lifted the cart onto the road. But at bat Gibson got off to a slow start, as his team languished in last place and he himself could manage only one home run in the opening weeks. In Santurce's first game against Guayama, Paige shut them out, and the opposition blew them away by a score of 23–0, as Gibson managed only one single in four at-bats.

Three weeks later the teams met again, and Paige triumphed easily, 6–1, again stopping Gibson with one single in four tries. In the third face-off, Santurce battled for 12 innings before losing 3–1, as Gibson got his customary 1-for-4. Finally, Paige beat Santurce again, 4–2, and this time Gibson went hitless. In four games, Satch had held him to a .188 batting average.

However, Gibson did much better against the other hurlers in the league, who included his Grays teammates Brown and Partlow. Gibson slowly raised his average to .389, only three points behind Cepeda, the league leader. His home run total also climbed to 6—one of them a 450-footer—enough to lead the league but still a low number for Gibson. Meanwhile, Paige kept winning. By season's end he sported a 19-3 record with an earned run average of 1.93. His long slump was apparently over.

The Americans loved Puerto Rico. They played three games a week on Saturday and Sunday. The

In 1940, Gibson skipped the Negro leagues season entirely to play for a team in Veracruz, Mexico. He clouted 11 home runs in 22 games during the Mexican season while batting .467.

rest of the week they were free, and the fans invited them to dinner and showered them with parties. They could hang around the bars in the plazas, and the people would not let them pay for anything.

Second baseman Dick Seay was Gibson's teammate on Santurce. "He went haywire," Seay said. After a game, the two would go to Gibson's home for a "tub of beer" and something to eat, then they'd "hit the hot spots." The next morning, Gibson would wake Seay up at dawn and say, "Come on, let's go to the *picarina* [tavern]. In the bars, Seay noticed that Gibson would spend long periods in the men's room, then come out "talking simple like." "What's wrong with the fellow?" Seay wondered. He guessed that Gibson was smoking marijuana.

One night, after a drinking bout, Gibson went down to the main plaza and began taking off his clothes. The police came and wrestled him into a paddy wagon. "He ripped the spare tire right off the back of the wagon," Seay recalled. "He was a strong man, just a big, big kid." Gibson did not play at all the final weeks of the season, and Seay had to don the catching gear himself.

Gibson did not go back to the Grays in 1940. He could make more money playing in Venezuela that spring—$700 a month plus a $1,000 bonus. When Mexican millionaire Jorge Pasquel offered him $6,000 to play in Mexico for the summer, Gibson snapped that up too. So did a lot of other Negro league stars such as Cool Papa Bell, Ray Dandridge, Bill Wright, Bill Byrd, and others. Back home, in the segregated United States, the players felt that they were "going in the back door," but in Latin America they were treated like royalty. Fans besieged them for autographs, and newspapers ran their pictures on page one.

Gibson played for Veracruz on the coast, but in Mexico City, where the air was thin, a batted ball could sail for miles. In all, Gibson blasted 11 homers in 22 games, knocked in 38 runs, and batted .467. Oddly, he did not lead the league in homers. The champion was Cool Papa Bell, the famous base stealer.

While Gibson was enjoying the good life in Latin America, back home Paige was suddenly becoming a celebrity. *Life* magazine and the *Saturday Evening Post* discovered him and ran pictures and stories that reached hundreds of thousands of readers, white as well as black. The publicity put Paige on the same pedestal with the nation's most famous black athletes, heavyweight champion Joe Louis and the 1936 Olympic track champion Jesse Owens. For the first time, said Ric Roberts, a white magazine "had burned incense at the foot of a black man outside the prize ring." And Paige cashed in on it. Crowds that used to average 3,000 a game suddenly swelled to 10 times that figure when Paige pitched.

Meanwhile, the Grays did not seem to miss Gibson. Ray Brown had perhaps the greatest year of any pitcher in Negro league history, with a record of 24-4 in a season less than half as long as the white big leagues played. Brown shattered the mark for the most victories in a single Negro league season as the Grays won their fourth pennant in a row.

The next summer, 1941, Posey offered Gibson a contract for $500 a month for four months, which Posey claimed was the highest salary ever offered to a black player. But Pasquel jumped in with an even better deal—$800 a month for eight months. Naturally, Gibson took the higher offer and jumped the Grays again, and all Posey could do was sue him for breach of contract.

Ray Brown also deserted his father-in-law to join Gibson in Veracruz, along with future Hall of Famer Ray Dandridge. Many Mexican fans consider the 1941 Veracruz team the greatest in history, Mexico's equivalent of the 1927 New York Yankees.

Gibson hit 33 homers in 358 at-bats, or about one home run every 10 times up. He struck out only 25 times—in other words, he had more home runs than strikeouts. (Today, some players have five or six strikeouts for every home run.) His batting average was .374. Most amazing of all, Gibson batted in 124

Gibson accepts his Most Valuable Player Award from the president of the Mexican League in 1941. Leading a Veracruz team that is considered the best in Mexican baseball history, Gibson drove in an astonishing 124 runs in only 94 games.

Though Gibson had a tendency to gain weight as he entered his thirties, the extra poundage failed to diminish his prowess at the plate.

runs in 94 games. At that pace, in a modern 162-game schedule, he would drive in over 200 runs a year.

After the Mexican season ended, Gibson was off to Puerto Rico to face a challenge from a new slugging star, Willard "Home Run" Brown of the Kansas City Monarchs. Many Monarchs players felt that Brown was an even better player than another man who came to the team four years later—Jackie Robinson. "He could outrun and outhit anybody in our league," one Kansas City player said. "He could jet when he wanted to run," another remarked.

Brown had arms as thick as tree trunks, and in 1947, at the age of 35, he obtained a tryout with the major league St. Louis Browns. Although he did not stay with the team, partly because of his age, he went on to set home run records in the minor leagues. That winter, Gibson and Brown met face-to-face in a showdown for the Puerto Rican batting title. Brown took the early lead, .441 to .335. A week later Brown was still ahead, .456 to .412. By February, Gibson had shot into the lead, .460 to .402. Gibson went on to finish with .480 and lead the league in home runs as well. In the half century since then, none of the great hitters playing winter ball in Puerto Rico—including Clemente, Cepeda, Willie Mays, or Tony Oliva—ever matched Gibson's average. •◑•

YELLOW CAB
HOBART 1212
AT BAT
STRIKES
BALLS
OUTS
SHAH & SHAH
JEWELERS 921 F ST. SILVERSMITHS
Dr Pepper
Wilson
SPORTS EQUIPMENT
BARKER
LUMBER & MILLWORK
NATIONAL 1348
ORIENTA
COFFEE
MIKE MARTIN'S
SNOW
GIBSON

8

FALSE HOPES

IN DECEMBER 1941, Japanese forces bombed the U.S. naval base at Pearl Harbor, Hawaii, and the United States was suddenly thrust into the biggest war of its history. Gibson was 30 years old and was not called up for military service. But he decided not to go to Mexico again for the 1942 season, staying with the Grays instead.

As the major league season opened, the Chicago White Sox gave a tryout to a black athlete best known for his exploits as a halfback with the University of California at Los Angeles (UCLA) football team. At the tryout, Jackie Robinson showed that he was at least as good at baseball as he was at football. He smacked line drives all over the field and raced around the bases. "He stole everything but my infielders' gloves," said manager Jimmy Dykes. At the end of the tryout, White Sox officials shook Robinson's hand and thanked him for coming out. He never heard from them again.

In Chicago that May, Satchel Paige and his Monarchs went up against Dizzy Dean and a team of

Gibson rounds third base in a 1943 game against the Baltimore Elite Giants at Washington's Griffith Stadium. Though Gibson continued to play brilliantly during the early 1940s, he suffered increasingly from the effects of drinking and drug abuse.

major leaguers who were in military service. The game drew 31,000 fans, while across town only 19,000 attended a White Sox doubleheader. The *Daily Worker*, a Communist party newspaper, began a campaign to open the major leagues to black players. The paper quoted Leo Durocher, then manager of the Dodgers, as saying, "I'll play the colored boys on my team if the big shots give the OK. Hell, I've seen a million good ones." The baseball commissioner, Judge Kenesaw Mountain Landis, called Durocher into his office. Landis had long been adamant in barring blacks from the majors, and he clearly gave Durocher a dressing down. When Durocher emerged from Landis's office, he said that he had been misquoted. But Landis still insisted that there was no rule, "formal or informal," against blacks playing in the white majors.

The black newspapers seized on the quote. LANDIS CLEARS WAY FOR OWNERS TO HIRE COLORED, proclaimed a headline in the Washington *Afro-American*. Black reporters rushed to interview white stars. One Pirate immortal of earlier years, Honus Wagner, said, "I've seen any number of Negro players who could be in the major leagues." Many others agreed with him.

The last-place Phillies reportedly wanted to sign Campanella, a Philadelphia native. Another report said the Cleveland Indians might offer a tryout to several members of the Negro league Cleveland Buckeyes.

The *Daily Worker* tried to get a tryout for Campanella with the Pirates. Though nothing came of it, Pittsburgh owner Bill Benswanger told the press, "We will give any man, white or colored, a chance when asked. . . . Colored players are American citizens with American rights. I know there are still many problems of traveling and playing to be ironed out, but after all, somebody has to make the first move."

Some white newspaper columnists, such as Bill Cunningham of the *Boston Herald*, wrote, "Let's give 'em a chance—let 'em up here and let's see if they can hit." But the baseball establishment remained unmoved. The baseball bible, the *Sporting News*, remarked in an editorial: "There's no law against Negroes playing with white teams, [but] the leaders of both groups know their crowd psychology and do not care to run the risk of damaging their own game."

Larry MacPhail, owner of the Brooklyn Dodgers, called the whole thing "100 percent hypocrisy." No colored player would ever play for the Dodgers, he vowed. He favored a long minor league apprenticeship for young black hopefuls until "they show their ability and character." When Judy Johnson asked Connie Mack, longtime owner of the Philadelphia Athletics, why the white owners would not accept black players, Mack replied, "Judy, there are just too many of you."

When a *Daily Worker* reporter came into the Grays dressing room asking the players to sign a petition demanding entry into the majors, Buck Leonard told him, "We're going to leave that to you all to discuss. We're going to play ball. Any writing you want done, you go ahead and do it. We're not out here to demonstrate or anything like that." From the standpoint of later times, his attitude might be difficult to understand, but American society was quite different in 1942. As Leonard himself said years later, when he and Gibson were inducted into the Hall of Fame at Cooperstown: "[The idea of integration] was as foreign to us as a man walking on the moon. . . . We thought the way things were was the way things were always going to be." It was also dangerous for a black to say anything to anger whites: Lynchings were still common news items in the daily papers.

Most black players scoffed at reports that the

Roy Campanella, later a Hall of Fame catcher with the Brooklyn and Los Angeles Dodgers, was one of the rising stars of the Negro leagues during the early 1940s. Campanella described Gibson as "not only the greatest catcher but the greatest ballplayer I ever saw."

Washington Senators owner Calvin Griffith (right), shown here with Hall of Fame pitcher Walter Johnson, flirted with the idea of integrating his struggling team during the early 1940s. However, most of his fellow owners opposed the idea, and baseball remained segregated until 1947.

owners would be willing to give them a chance. But Gibson thought the owners were sincere. "Aw," he said, "I don't believe they'd kid about a serious thing like that."

In fact, Senators owner Clark Griffith had been thinking the subject over carefully. His team had not won a pennant in 10 years and was deep in the second division. The Senators had become a national joke: "Washington, first in war, first in peace, and last in the American League." Finally, Griffith called Gibson and Leonard into his office. "You all played a good ball game today," he said. "You fellows got good size on you, and it looked like you were playing to win. Ric Roberts is talking about getting you fellows on the Senators' team. Well, let me tell you something. If we get you boys, we're gonna get the best ones. It's gonna break up your league. Now what do you think about that?"

"Well," Leonard said, "we'd be happy to play in the major leagues and believe we could make the team." Neither he nor Gibson ever heard from Griffith again.

In the end, the talk of integration petered out. Gibson remained with the Grays, who were winning their sixth pennant in a row, more than any U.S. team has ever won before or since. Contemplating Gibson's position, Honus Wagner shook his head sadly. "[Josh Gibson is] one of the best natural hitters I've ever seen," he said, "but it's too late for the majors now."

If Gibson was hurt and angry, he took it out on the ball. That year he batted .335 and led the league with 15 homers. At the East-West game in August, he stepped up against Satchel Paige, renewing their classic rivalry. With men on second and third, Paige decided to walk Gibson and pitch to Bill Wright, who slapped into a double play. In the ninth, Gibson came up again with men on second and third and first base open, and again Paige refused to pitch to him, although this time Wright singled in two runs to give the East the victory.

A month later, Gibson and Paige met again in the World Series. The night before the Series opened, the two sat at opposite ends of the bar in Greenlee's Crawford Grille, boasting loudly of what each was going to do to the other in the game the next day. Meanwhile, the light-hitting Monarchs shortstop, Jesse Williams, decided to psyche Gibson a little. "Sit down here, Josh," he said, offering to bet the big guy a steak on which player would outhit the other.

"You see this bat?" Gibson said.

"Yeah," Jesse nodded.

"That's my bat. I don't break 'em, I *wear* 'em out."

But in Game 1, Paige and his reliever allowed only two hits, and Willard Brown blasted a 435-foot triple, as the Monarchs won 8–0. Two nights later, on a damp night in Philadelphia, Paige and Gibson squared off again in one of the great dramas of baseball history.

Paige came in to relieve with a two-run lead when the Grays lead-off man singled. Paige calmly gave an intentional walk to the next man, Vic Harris, then began to walk Howard Easterling as well. Manager Frank Duncan and owner J. L. Wilkinson ran out

Gibson trots home with a run against the Newark Eagles in 1942. Among the highlights of the Negro league season was the epic confrontation between Gibson and Paige in Game 1 of the black World Series—Paige struck out the great slugger on three straight pitches.

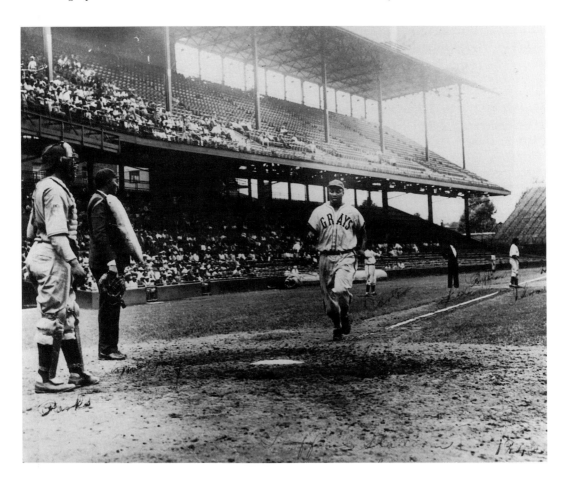

onto the field. "What, are you crazy?" they demanded. "Josh is up next!" But Paige just shooed them away. "OK," they said, walking away and shaking their heads. "It's your funeral."

"The bases were drunk," Paige later recalled. "And there was Josh up there."

"I tell you what I'm gonna do," Paige called to Gibson. "I'm not gonna trick you. I'm gonna give you a good fastball." Paige wound up and, as he recalled, "stuck my foot way up in the air. It hid the ball and almost hid me too. Then I fired."

The pitch was indeed a fastball, right at the knees. Gibson took it for strike one. "Now," Paige announced, "I'm gonna throw you another fastball, only it's gonna be a little faster than the other." He then delivered strike two.

"One more to go," Paige wrote in his autobiography. "I knew it. Josh knew it. The crowd knew it. It was so tense, you could feel everything tingling." The third pitch was a three-quarter sidearm curve ball. Gibson, looking for another fastball, rocked back on his heels. Strike three.

"How's that, big man?" Satchel laughed. But Gibson would not reply. Wrote Paige: "Josh tossed his bat 4,000 feet and stomped off the field." He would later call it "the best day I ever had pitching."

Paige and the Kansas City pitchers held Gibson to a .125 batting average for the Series and swept it in four straight. The most frustrating year in Gibson's life had come to an end. ❧

9
CHANGING TIMES

ON NEW YEAR'S DAY, 1943, Gibson fainted, went into a coma, and was rushed to a hospital. Doctors said he had suffered a nervous breakdown. Gibson himself later claimed he had a brain tumor, but he refused to permit an operation. There followed a season of severe mental and emotional troubles. Gibson picked fights with bartenders. On one occasion, he climbed nude onto a window ledge six stories high and threatened to jump.

Some of his teammates blamed liquor, but Leonard and others thought otherwise. "I think it was dope," said Grays pitcher Wilmer "Red" Fields. The players were invited to parties in every city they visited, and Fields believed that Gibson picked up the habit from the high-living partygoers. In addition, Gibson had a new girlfriend, a woman whose husband was serving in the army. She was known to be a drug user, and another teammate said, "What she was taking, he was taking."

Gibson spent the summer going in and out of Washington's St. Elizabeth Hospital "like a drunken monkey," according to Leonard. At one point, Gibson was committed for 10 days under heavy sedation, with his arms immobilized by a straitjacket. But he was so strong he literally ripped the jacket off. He played ball on weekends, attended by hospital orderlies.

Gibson's expression in this 1943 photograph conveys the moodiness and emotional instability that afflicted him at this time. Despite his personal difficulties, he finished the season with an astonishing .517 batting average.

Yet that year Gibson batted an amazing .517. Only one man in Negro league history had ever hit better than that—John Henry Lloyd, with a .564 average in 1928. Gibson also slugged 16 homers, the most he had ever hit in one year, plus 23 doubles. He batted in 59 runs in only 190 at-bats: in a 162-game season, that would would amount to about 240 RBIs. (The major league single-season record is 190.) Ten of Gibson's homers came in cavernous Griffith Stadium, where only three home runs were hit into the left-field bleachers in 77 American League games that year.

Sweetest of all to Gibson was the revenge he gained against Satchel Paige. During a game in Chicago's Comiskey Park, Paige recalled, "I got my fastball in a little too high. He hit it so hard, it hit the top deck and bounced back in the ball park. He could hit home runs around Babe Ruth's home runs."

The white press began to recognize Gibson at last. *Time* magazine did a picture story on him, calling Gibson "a very dark Babe Ruth." *Time* said many white fans came out to the Negro league games to see "the fancy windups, the swift and daring base running, and the flashy one-handed catches." The Grays often drew larger crowds than the Senators, the magazine said. It reported that Gibson earned only $750 a month, or about $3,000 for the four-month season, a far cry from the salaries Ruth had earned.

As U.S. industry mobilized for the war effort, jobs became plentiful. The nation finally emerged from the Great Depression, and the Negro leagues benefited. One day the Senators played in Griffith Stadium before 3,000 fans, while that same night the Grays and Monarchs drew 30,000. "Even the white folks was coming out," Paige said. "They'd heard about Josh and me."

At the East-West game, which drew over 50,000 people each year, the players were paid $50 each,

Gibson in action behind the plate in a contest against the Newark Eagles. During the war years, Gibson's prodigious talents finally began to draw national recognition; but as he approached his mid-thirties, his chances of playing in the white major leagues were diminishing.

while the owners made enough profits from that one game to cover their losses for the rest of the season. Paige concluded that without him and Gibson, the game would not draw 20,000 fans. He decided to ask for more money and told Gibson, "They got to come through with some extra money for us if we both hold out." Satch suggested that they demand $200 each.

The league president "almost fell out of his chair," Paige recalled. But he and Gibson got their money. A year later, the rest of the players also demanded $200 apiece, and when the owners refused, the players threatened to strike. They got their raises, thanks to the ground Gibson and Paige had broken.

The Grays won the pennant again in 1943, their seventh straight, and this time met the Birmingham Black Barons in the World Series. Gibson was held to a .263 average, though he slugged a grand slam and had a key hit in the rally that won the fifth and final game.

Gibson's magnificent and tragic season was summed up by a story told by Grays shortstop Sammy Bankhead. One day, Bankhead observed Gibson sitting alone by his rooming house window, having an imaginary conversation. "C'mon, Joe, talk to me," Gibson was mumbling. "Why don't you talk to me? Heh, Joe DiMaggio, it's me. You know me. Why don't you answer me? Huh, Joe? Why not? C'mon, Joe, you know me. You ain't gonna answer me?"

That winter, Gibson stayed in Pittsburgh. Cum Posey asked Ted Page to watch out for Gibson, and the two friends went bowling and played handball and volleyball at the YMCA. But next spring, Gibson was in trouble again for "breaking training." In an exhibition doubleheader at Brooklyn's Ebbets Field, home of the Dodgers, he was in no shape to play, but Posey put him in anyway, because the fans were begging for him. He went 1-for-9.

During the 1944 Negro league season, Gibson batted .361 with a league-leading 6 homers. Roy Campanella, by comparison, batted .344. Sam Jethroe, who would later play in the white majors with the Boston Braves, led the Western league with a .353 average. The Grays won their eighth pennant in a row, and again they beat Birmingham in five games in the World Series. Gibson did much better this time, batting an even .500, including a long home run in Birmingham's spacious Rickwood Field. Two months later, the white baseball commissioner, Judge Landis, died, setting off perhaps the most profound revolution in the game's history.

The new commissioner, Albert "Happy" Chandler, was a U.S. senator from Kentucky. Upon Chandler's appointment to the commissioner's job, Ric Roberts and other black reporters rushed to Chandler's office in the Capitol to interview him. They asked him point-blank if he would let black players in the majors. Chandler had just returned from a tour of the Pacific war zone, where many African-American soldiers (still segregated from white troops) had fought and died for their country. "If a boy can make it on Guadalcanal and Okinawa, hell, he can make it in baseball," Chandler said. He added: "Once I tell you something, pardner, I never change. You can count on me." This was the green light that Branch Rickey, general manager of the Brooklyn

Dodgers, had been waiting for. He began making plans to integrate his ballclub.

Meanwhile, as the war in Europe ended in the spring of 1945, Gibson and Leonard pulled a double holdout. They threatened to play in Mexico if Posey did not raise their salaries. The Grays owner eventually agreed to pay Leonard $1,000 a month and raise Gibson to $1,200. Although Gibson's new salary amounted to less than $5,000 for the four-month season, it made him the second-highest-paid black player in America, after Paige.

Brooklyn scouts were quietly joining the crowds at Negro league games. Rickey had ordered them to look for "a man that possesses more than talent, a man who can carry the burden of abuse on the field, a man to wear the badge of martyrdom, a man whose humility and courage would force the press to accept him." Unknown to them, Paige and Gibson had already been considered and rejected, Paige as too old and Gibson as too unstable.

Paige was having the worst season of his career, with only 3 wins and 4 losses, as the Monarchs had lost most of their stars to the military draft. But they did sign one new shortstop, a college boy just out of the army. "I'd never heard of him before," Paige wrote. "But he was pretty good—quick on his feet

Black artillerymen position a 155-millimeter howitzer during a 1944 battle on the European front. Throughout World War II, the U.S. armed forces were still segregated; but the heroism of black soldiers helped convince the nation that racial separation— in the military, in sports, and in other walks of life—was intolerable.

and good hands at the plate." The new player was the former football star who had been given a brief tryout with the White Sox before he entered the army—Jackie Robinson.

In June, the Monarchs traveled east to play a doubleheader against the Grays, and Gibson got his first look at the new man. The Monarchs coach knew that Robinson had dreams of the major leagues, but he feared that Robinson did not have a strong enough arm to play shortstop. He asked the Grays' Cool Papa Bell to hit some balls to Robinson's right. Robinson reached the balls, but he could not plant his right foot well enough to make the long throw from the hole, and Bell was safe every time.

In the first game, Robinson's fielding problems continued. The game was tied, 2–2, with the bases loaded, when Gibson drilled one of Paige's pitches to the shortstop. Robinson fielded the ball and whipped it home—over the catcher's head. Two men scored, and five more followed before the inning was over. But at bat Robinson was perfect: 7-for-7. He went on to bat .387 for the year.

After the game, Bell went up to the rookie and urged him to try another infield position. The advice took, because in his 11 years in the major leagues, Robinson played only one game at shortstop.

Although hobbled by a leg ailment, plus his various substance-abuse problems, Gibson hit .375 and again led the league in homers with eight, the sixth straight year he had been home run king. His last homer went over the high roof of New York's Polo Grounds, a blow estimated at 500 feet. Players reported that Gibson was still drinking heavily, and he was benched in the East-West game for "breaking training" once again.

In August 1945, as the war in the Pacific was finally coming to an end with the surrender of Japan, the Grays won their ninth straight pennant and

prepared to play the World Series against the Cleveland Buckeyes, led by Jethroe, the West's top hitter
at .393. Gibson hit .316 with 11 homers. In the
World Series, the Grays faltered as the Buckeyes
swept them in four straight, holding Gibson to a .133
batting average.

That winter, Gibson was in Puerto Rico when the
stunning news was announced: Robinson had been
signed to a Brooklyn Dodgers contract. Gibson re-
acted with pain and bewilderment. As Ric Roberts
recalled, "Most people don't realize what pride Josh
took in being 'Mr. Black Baseball.' He thought, if
they're going to pick a black man, it had to be Josh
Gibson. How they could pick Jackie Robinson was
something he could never understand. To find his
kingdom in a shambles at the age of 33 was too much
for him. He turned to everything he could find—dope
and everything."

That winter in Puerto Rico, a despondent Gibson
hit only .190 with no home runs. Police arrested him
when they found him wandering nude in downtown
San Juan and committed him to a sanitarium.

Despite his close association with Gibson, Buck
Leonard agreed that Robinson was the right man to
be first. "Josh wouldn't have taken the heckling
Jackie took in the majors," Buck said. "He would have
blown his top." Satchel Paige was also brokenhearted
that he had been passed over, although in later years
he would admit, "Jackie was the right guy. I'm glad
it wasn't me, because I couldn't have taken it either."

Robinson got the news the night before he em-
barked for Venezuela with Buck Leonard. On the
tour, Robinson batted .281, and Leonard hit .425.
Robinson was worried that he could not make the
majors and confided his fears to his roommate, Gene
Benson. "Jackie," Benson said, "just remember one
thing: Where you're goin' ain't half as tough as where
you been." ❧

Photo By
ERNEST C WITHERS
OF MEMPHIS 46

10

"ROARING TOWARD HIS END"

❧

GIBSON AND PAIGE were virtually forgotten men as the 1946 baseball season opened. All the black fans and black newspapers were focused on Montreal, where Jackie Robinson was playing with the Royals, the Dodgers' top farm team. The Dodgers had also signed Grays pitcher Johnny Wright, Baltimore catcher Roy Campanella, and Newark pitcher Don Newcombe. They did not pay the black teams anything for these players. Cum Posey, who died in March, raved at Rickey's nerve in "coming into a man's store and stealing the merchandise right off the shelves."

Gibson's two children, now in their teens, often came to the park with their grandmother to ask for money. Gibson's girlfriend also dropped him and went back to her husband. These problems may have contributed to his increased drinking. A photo of Gibson taken that summer showed an out-of-shape man who had ballooned to 230 pounds. He could barely squat down behind the plate and was so slow afoot that he turned doubles into singles. And yet this overweight, arthritic, alcoholic shell of the old Josh Gibson had a spectacular season that surpassed even his heroic production of 1943. As in the earlier year, he seemed to smash the ball with a savagery that released his pent-up frustration.

Gibson looks wary as he poses for photographers before the 1946 East-West Game. Though enjoying another successful season, the great catcher was in the throes of a mental and physical decline that would end with his death the following winter.

Montreal Royals officials watch Jackie Robinson sign his first professional contract in October 1945. Though Josh Gibson was unquestionably the greatest player in the Negro leagues, Brooklyn general manager Branch Rickey believed that Gibson was too unstable to handle the abuse that he would have to endure from white fans and players.

Still, few people paid attention. The headlines were all about Robinson, while Gibson and the Grays were relegated to the bottom of the page. For example, the April 6 *Afro-American* headline screamed: 50,000 SEE ROBINSON SPARKLE IN FIRST 6 GAMES. Below the headline was a large picture of Robinson crossing the plate after his first home run. On May 11, the paper proclaimed: MONTREAL FANS GREET JACKIE WITH WILD ACCLAIM. At the foot of the page, the paper noted, "Gibson Homers as Grays, Win, Lose."

A week later, Gibson hit a titanic shot in Forbes Field. The ball was reportedly 100 feet up in the air as it cleared the center-field fence, 457 feet away. But the headlines read: ROBINSON LEADS INTERNATIONAL LEAGUE IN BATTING. When Gibson replied with a smash into the center-field bleachers at Yankee Stadium, there were no pictures or headlines to mark the feat, only a small box midway down the sports page.

In addition to Robinson, Gibson had another rival, heavyweight boxing champion Joe Louis. When Louis knocked out challenger Billy Conn on June 15, the *Afro-American* proclaimed JOE KEEPS TITLE in two-inch-high letters and filled its sports pages with huge photos and details of the fight. No one seemed to care that Gibson had driven a ball into a stiff wind and over the roof of Philadelphia's Shibe Park. "What about *me?*" Gibson seemed to be crying. But no one listened.

In St. Louis's Sportsman's Park, Gibson hit a ball clear over the bleachers to the right of the center-field scoreboard, a drive estimated variously at 450 to 540 feet. The *Afro-American* ignored the blow entirely, reporting only that the former Negro leaguer Roy Partlow had been released by the Royals and that "tan pitcher" Don Newcombe, on the other hand, was enjoying a sensational season with the team.

Gibson finished the Negro league season with the amazing total of 16 home runs in only 132 at-bats, or one homer for every 8.3 at-bats. In 1927, when Babe Ruth hit 60 home runs, he had averaged 1 every 9 times up. In 1961, when Roger Maris hit 61, he averaged 1 every 9.7 at-bats. If Gibson had maintained his 1946 pace over the same number of at-bats Maris had (590), he would have hit 71 home runs. He also batted .379, second only to the .397 of Newark's Larry Doby, who would go on to the Cleveland Indians in 1948. Doby and teammate Monte Irvin powered the Eagles to the pennant, ending the Grays' nine-year winning streak.

That winter, Gibson was often found in a dreary Pittsburgh bar, drinking and brooding. His weight had fallen alarmingly, down to 180 pounds. Ted Page found him one day shaking another customer by the collar. "Tell him who hit the longest ball anywhere," he called to Page. "Tell him!"

On a cold Saturday night, January 20, 1947, Page bumped into Gibson again, this time on a windy street corner. "He was like always, full of play and kidding around," Page recalled. The two wrestled playfully before parting. In *Only the Ball Was White*, Robert Peterson has given the following account of what happened next:

> Josh came home and told his mother that he felt sick. He said that he believed he was going to have a stroke. Mrs. Gibson said, "Shush, Josh, you're not going to have no stroke," but she sent him to bed. The family gathered around his bedside and waited for a doctor while Josh laughed and talked. Then he sent his brother Jerry to the homes of friends to collect his scattered trophies and his radio and bring them home. "So Jerry came back about ten-thirty," Mrs. Mahaffey said, "and we were all laughing and talking, and then he had a stroke. He just got through laughing and then he raised up in the bed and went to talk, but you couldn't understand

Robinson tears up the basepaths during the 1947 season, in which he batted .297 and led the National League in stolen bases. After the season, he was named rookie of the year for both major leagues.

what he was saying. Then he lay back down and died right off."

Just three months, later Jackie Robinson walked onto a big league field in a Brooklyn Dodger uniform, through the door that Josh Gibson had helped break down but was never allowed to walk through.

Gibson's sudden death at the age of 35 was more than a personal tragedy. It was also a tragedy for baseball, because most American fans were denied the chance to see one of the game's greatest hitters. "He would have been a superstar in the majors," Ted Page maintained. If Gibson had been able to wait, as Satchel Paige waited, he almost surely would have gone to the Cleveland Indians as Paige's catcher in 1948.

Gibson was buried in a numbered grave in Pittsburgh's Allegheny Cemetery. Twenty-eight years later, Ted Page found the grave overgrown with weeds and began a fund drive to buy a headstone. Willie Stargell of the Pirates was the first to contribute, and the baseball commissioner's office covered the rest.

Recalling his old friend, Ric Roberts said, "We used to talk a lot about blacks going into the major leagues, and Josh said to me, 'I'll believe it when I see it.' " Roberts composed a piece he called "Memo to Josh Gibson," describing to his dead friend the revolutionary changes that had come over the game since the days "when Josh Gibson was roaring toward his end."

The reasons for Gibson's untimely death are still a matter of speculation. There are those who believe the fatal stroke was caused by a drug overdose. "I refuse to say that Josh destroyed himself," Ted Page declared. "Some people say Josh Gibson died of a brain hemmorhage. I say he died of a broken heart."

Josh Gibson, Jr., and Baseball Commissioner Bowie Kuhn hold a replica of Josh Gibson's Hall of Fame plaque during ceremonies at Cooperstown, New York, in the summer of 1972.

Whatever brought about his end, Gibson's memory remained vivid to those who had known him and seen him play. When Roy Campanella entered the Hall of Fame in 1969, the second black man, after Jackie Robinson, to be so honored, he protested to reporters, "I couldn't carry Josh Gibson's glove. Anything I could do, he could do better."

Three years later, in 1972, Josh Gibson joined Campanella and Robinson in Cooperstown, voted in by a special committee on Negro league veterans. (Satchel Paige, inducted in 1971, had been the first Negro leaguer to enter the Hall of Fame.) Buck Leonard was elected at the same time, and at the induction ceremonies, he spoke for Gibson and the other Negro leaguers as well as for himself. Though barred from the major leagues, Leonard said, "we felt we were contributing something to baseball too. We played with a round ball and round bats, and we loved it—because there wasn't that much money in it." Getting into Cooperstown, Leonard remarked, "is something I never thought would happen."

Josh Gibson, Jr., 42 years old, accepted the plaque for his father. Josh junior had gone through the gate his father never could enter; he played briefly in the low minors in 1951 for Farnham of the Provincial League under manager Sammy Bankhead, his father's old buddy on the Grays.

"I want to say a personal word to my father," Josh junior told Commissioner Bowie Kuhn on the rostrum:

"Wake up, Dad, you just made it in." ◆

APPENDIX:
CAREER STATISTICS †

―――――― ❦ ――――――

HOMESTEAD GRAYS, PITTSBURGH CRAWFORDS, WASHINGTON HOMESTEAD GRAYS

YEAR	TEAM	G	AB	H	2B	3B	HR	SB	BA
1930	HOM	10	33	8	1	0	1	1	.242
1931		32	129	48	8	0	6*	0	.272
1932	PIT	46	147	42	3	5*	7	1	.286
1933		34	116	42	8	1	6	1	.362
1934		41	146	46	8*	3	11*	1	.315
1935		37	129	43	7	1	11*	3	.333
1936		23	75	27	3	0	11*	0	.360
1937	HOM	12	42	21	0	4*	7	0	.500
1938		19	74	23	1	0	4	1	.311
1939	WAS	29	88	29	2	2	17*	0	.330
1940◆		2	6	1	0	0	1	0	.167
1942	WAS	51	158	53	8	1	15*	3	.335
1943		57	209	108	23*	8*	16*	0	.517
1944		28	97	35	3	3	6*	0	.361
1945		31	98	31	3	3	11	0	.316
1946		49	132	50	11*	4	16*	0	.379
Totals		501	1679	607	89	35	146	11	.362

* Led League
◆ Played in Latin America during most of 1940 and 1941

---

† These statistics cover only the official Negro league games in which Gibson appeared. No statistics were recorded for the numerous games his teams played against semiprofessional teams nor for the games he played against major leaguers during barnstorming tours.

CHRONOLOGY

—— ❦ ——

1911	Born Joshua Gibson in Buena Vista, Georgia, on December 21
1924	Gibson family resettles in Pittsburgh, Pennsylvania
1927	Gibson goes to work in Pittsburgh steel mill and plays amateur baseball with Gimbels A.C.
1929	Begins to play for Crawford Colored Giants, a black semipro team
1930	Signs with the Homestead Grays of the Negro National League; plays in first game on July 25; hits legendary home run at Yankee Stadium on September 27
1931	Plays first full season for the Grays; leads Negro National League in home runs
1932–36	Signs with Pittsburgh Crawfords; leads Negro National League in home runs three times in five seasons while batting .331
1937	Begins season with Trujillo Dragones (Dragons) in the Dominican Republic; returns to Homestead Grays and hits 7 home runs in 12 games while batting .500
1939	Hits 17 home runs in 29 games to lead Negro National League
1940–41	Plays in Puerto Rico and Mexico; drives in 124 runs in 94 games while playing for Veracruz
1942	Returns to Homestead Grays, leading league with 15 home runs
1943	Hits 16 home runs in 57 games while batting .517
1946	Plays final season, leading league in doubles and home runs despite increasing physical and emotional problems
1947	Dies in Pittsburgh, Pennsylvania, on January 20; Jackie Robinson makes debut with the Brooklyn Dodgers, breaking baseball's color line
1972	Gibson is enshrined in the National Baseball Hall of Fame in Cooperstown, New York

FURTHER READING

Bruce, Janet. *The Kansas City Monarchs: Champions of Black Baseball*. Lawrence: University Press of Kansas, 1985.

Holway, John B. *Blackball Stars: Negro League Pioneers*. New York: Carroll & Graf, 1992.

———. *Black Diamonds*. Westport, CT: Meckler, 1989.

———. *Josh and Satch: The Life and Times of Josh Gibson and Satchel Paige*. New York: Carroll & Graf, 1992.

———. *Voices from the Great Black Baseball Leagues*. New York: Dodd, Mead, 1975.

Peterson, Robert. *Only the Ball Was White: A History of Legendary Players and All-Black Professional Teams*. New York: Oxford University Press, 1970.

Riley, James A. *Biographical Encyclopedia of the Negro Baseball Leagues*. New York: Carroll & Graf, 1994.

Rogosin, Donn. *Invisible Men: Life in Baseball's Negro Leagues*. New York: Atheneum, 1985.

Ruck, Rob. *Sandlot Seasons: Sport in Black Pittsburgh*. Champaign: University of Illinois Press, 1987.

Scott, Richard. *Jackie Robinson*. New York: Chelsea House, 1987.

Shirley, David. *Satchel Paige*. New York: Chelsea House, 1993.

Tygiel, Jules. *Baseball's Great Experiment: Jackie Robinson and His Legacy*. New York: Vintage, 1984.

INDEX

PICTURE CREDITS

JOHN B. HOLWAY became interested in the Negro leagues as a 15-year-old in 1945, when he saw Josh Gibson face Satchel Paige in Washington's Griffith Stadium. His first books, *Japan Is Big League in Thrills* and *Sumo*, were published in Tokyo in 1954 and 1955, respectively. Holway began writing about the history of black baseball in 1969, and his first book on the subject, *Voices from the Great Black Baseball Leagues*, appeared in 1975. He has since published three more books on the Negro leagues, plus innumerable articles on the subject for such publications as the *New York Times*, the *Washington Post*, *American Heritage*, and *TV Guide*. Holway's books on general baseball subjects include *The Pitcher*, (with John Thorn), *The Sluggers*, and *The Last .400 Hitter*. He has also contributed frequently to the *Sporting News*, *Baseball Weekly*, and other sports periodicals. On behalf of the U.S. Information Agency, he covered world economic news, the space program, and the 1968 and 1984 Olympics. Now retired, Holway resides in Springfield, Virginia.

NATHAN IRVIN HUGGINS, one of America's leading scholars in the field of black studies, helped select the titles for the BLACK AMERICANS OF ACHIEVEMENT series, for which he also served as senior consulting editor. He was the W.E.B. Du Bois Professor of History and of Afro-American Studies at Harvard University and the director of the W.E.B. Du Bois Institute for Afro-American Research at Harvard. He received his doctorate from Harvard in 1962 and returned there as a professor in 1980 after teaching at Columbia University, the University of Massachusetts, Lake Forest College, and the California State University, Long Beach. He was the author of four books and dozens of articles, including *Black Odyssey: The Afro-American Ordeal in Slavery*, *The Harlem Renaissance*, and *Slave and Citizen: The Life of Frederick Douglass*, and was associated with the Children's Television Workshop, National Public Radio, the Boston Athenaeum, the Museum of Afro-American History, the Howard Thurman Educational Trust, and Upward Bound. Professor Huggins died in 1989, at the age of 62, in Cambridge, Massachusetts.